BEFRIENDING

DEATH

Henri Nouwen and a
Spirituality of Dying

Michelle O'Rourke

ORBIS BOOKS
Maryknoll, New York 10545

Founded in 1970, Orbis Books endeavors to publish works that enlighten the mind, nourish the spirit, and challenge the conscience. The publishing arm of the Maryknoll Fathers and Brothers, Orbis seeks to explore the global dimensions of the Christian faith and mission, to invite dialogue with diverse cultures and religious traditions, and to serve the cause of reconciliation and peace. The books published reflect the views of their authors and do not represent the official position of the Maryknoll Society. To learn more about Maryknoll and Orbis Books, please visit our website at www.maryknollsociety.org.

Manufactured in the United States of America

Library of Congress Cataloging-in-Publication Data

O'Rourke, Michelle.
  Befriending death : Henri Nouwen and a spirituality of dying / Michelle O'Rourke.
      p. cm.
  ISBN 978-1-57075-840-9 (pbk.)
  1. Death—Religious aspects—Catholic Church. 2. Nouwen, Henri J. M. I. Title.
  BT825.O67 2009
  242'.4—dc22
                                        2009022202

To my husband
Tom

whose unconditional love
and support reveals to me
the face of God.

Contents

Foreword

All of this is extremely difficult. Randy couldn't talk about his pain until I pushed him. Recently he admitted how, at age fifteen, his whole life was terribly affected when his father died and his mother was unable to cope. He's scared for Christopher, and so am I, because neither of us knows what we should and shouldn't tell him. I want to be honest with Chris so he knows that he can always trust me to tell him the truth.

This email from my niece Katie is about her dying husband, Randy, and their eight-year-old son, Christopher. It came while I was reading Michelle O'Rourke's manuscript for *Befriending Death.*

This was a true privilege—to be allowed an inside view of Michelle's rare experience of nursing in critical care and ministering in a large church, and to see that integrated so beautifully with the wisdom of Henri Nouwen's life and ministry. This book is a rare gift indeed.

Michelle examines our culture's flight from death and moves beyond that toward something entirely new—a compassionate embrace of death, the one inevitable reality that awaits us all. The many easy-to-identify-with stories from people who have "been there," as well as lessons on dying and how to care for the ill and dying are liberating and provide seldom-heard insights into living and dying.

Michelle describes befriending death as a positive movement, unrelated to the fear that surrounds this profoundly human experience. She frees us from the trepidation, dismay, and anxiety we inevitably experience when summoned to the bedside of a dying relative, or when faced with the friend whose spouse has just died in an accident, or when we hear a doctor's prognosis of a terminal illness. By befriending death we are liberated to live.

The reality of loss is also explored. Michelle explains the shattering of our illusions around needing to be in control when we are faced with sickness and our common vulnerability. She names our fears, then points us beyond toward a connection with other brothers and sisters who suffer within the same human family. She helps us to see how this solidarity offers a profound experience of being more fully human.

Not only does Michelle offer guidelines for "how to be with" very vulnerable people, she directs us to take care of ourselves as caregivers! Her advice to those giving care resonated deeply within me. *Don't be alone as the sole caregiver,* she tells us. *Rather, work to create a small community of people to surround and respond to the weakest in our midst.* By so doing we are gifting the ill person with more than one important relationship and providing space apart for ourselves to recuperate our energies for the long road.

Steadied by so much of what Michelle had to say, I was able to be direct with my niece. I told her: "My heart beats with yours when I hear you speak of your efforts to talk to Chris and Randy. . . . It seems to me that if he isn't too weak, perhaps Randy could consider having a father-son conversation with Chris. He could share about having the lung transplant when Chris was four, the infections, the terrible weakness, and the awful exercises, all of which he willingly lived because he wanted to be with Chris and watch him grow up. He could tell Chris that he may die soon, but Chris goes with him whatever occurs because he's so special and amazing—the best thing that ever happened to him. Randy can thank him for the joy and the happiness that he brought to his life in the past eight years. Most of all, Randy can tell Chris how much he loves him and why. Finally, Randy can ask Chris what he is feeling. They can cry together and you can go on from there with Christopher."

Just days before he died, Randy's heart-to-heart with Christopher more deeply sealed the bond of their love. It didn't relieve either of them of their unimaginable grief, but they were able to move forward with less angst because Katie posed the question—because I was reading this wonderful manuscript.

Befriending Death presents a deeply personal and universal vision into the human reality of death and dying. It is inviting, clear, hopeful, enlightening, liberating, and full of wisdom.

Sue Mosteller
Henri Nouwen Legacy Trust
March 2009

Acknowledgments

The completion of this work is a testament to the love and support I have received over the past two years. Tom, your selfless love kept me going, and our children, Matt, Sarah, Rebecca, and Katie, have very graciously listened as I talked endlessly about this project. I thank you and love you all so much!

Mary Ann Flanagan, IHM, your wisdom and guidance were invaluable, and I would never have accomplished this work without you. Cindy Waddick, your love and positive energy kept me going, as did your keen eye for editing! Fr. Bill McGrattan, thanks for your support and prayers and for allowing me time at the cottage for solitude and inspiration.

Many thanks to the wonderful people of St. Joseph Parish and to the parish palliative care volunteers who continue to inspire me. I hope this work will be fruitful in assisting you to minister to the sick and dying. Also, thanks to my coworkers in the emergency department who watched me spend hours on the night shift reading and writing, and always took time to ask me how things were going. We have journeyed together through many tragedies and deaths over the years, yet your care and concern for the patients and their loved ones is extraordinary. To you and to all of my colleagues serving in the Diocese of London, Ontario, I am grateful for your ongoing support and encouragement.

One of my greatest joys has been getting to know Henri Nouwen not only through my research but also in spending time with some of his friends. Sue Mosteller, I can't thank you enough for taking the time to meet with me, read my drafts, and gift me with your beautiful foreword. I am also grateful for the warm hospitality of the Daybreak Community during my visits there, and I thank the members of the Green House and the New House for having me for dinner. I also thank all of the people who allowed me to share their personal stories of Henri. It is truly an honor to be able to be a part of allowing his legacy to continue.

Thanks to Gabrielle Earnshaw and the staff of the Henri Nouwen Archives, the staff at the Henri Nouwen Society, and to my good friend Michael Hryniuk. I appreciated your expertise and support and assure you of mine as you continue to introduce others to Henri's writings. To Robert Ellsberg and the wonderful people at Orbis Books, I am forever indebted to you. When I began my thesis research, I had no idea it would someday end up in print. God never ceases to amaze me!

Finally, I thank my parents, Helen and George, and the rest of my family and friends for their continued love and support. The bonds we all share have given me strength and security in my own journey of living. In a special way I would like to dedicate this work to all those who are on a cancer journey. Maureen and Mark, your courage and faith inspire me. And dad, with your chemo behind you now, we are grateful for your continued health and how you model the way to live each day to the fullest.

May Henri's words give hope and strength to everyone who reads them!

Michelle O'Rourke

Introduction

As a lay pastoral minister in a large Roman Catholic urban parish and a practicing registered nurse, I have experienced many instances where both of my vocations or professions have naturally intersected. Fortunately, our society has come to understand that it is necessary to recognize physical, psychosocial, and spiritual needs in order to provide true holistic care to its members. Spending the last three decades nursing in critical care areas, much of that time spent in our local emergency department, has allowed me to be present as countless family members, friends, parishioners, and others have faced serious medical crises. Often the journey I walk with them is one of the most difficult for any person to take in experiencing the sudden or impending death of a loved one.

I am grateful for what I have learned from my colleagues, in both medicine and ministry, regarding how to navigate these difficult moments. I am also indebted to those who, through their own death or the death of their loved one, have shared with me their personal experience of facing this realm of the unknown. It is truly a sacred journey and an honor to accompany them.

Although I have often been present with the dying and their families, in a pastoral role, a health care role, or as a friend or family member, I have usually felt inadequate and unsure of how to address that "elephant in the room." There seemed to be no easy way to talk about dying. I suspect the same questions are faced by anyone in this situation: "How do you help someone face the end of his or her life? How do you watch someone die, and help the family do that as well? How do you help people pick up the pieces of a life to be lived without their loved one?"

Certainly, there are practical answers to the medical questions in how to provide necessary physical services, treatment, pain control, comfort measures, and so on. It seems the more difficult areas to talk about have to do with the psychosocial and spiritual elements of end-of-life care. These include addressing and accepting one's own dying, as well as the many bereavement and grief issues faced by those who live on.

In response to my own personal and professional desire to learn more about palliative care and spirituality, I began to search for answers. After attending some courses and workshops in the field, I eventually had the opportunity to work with a team of local experts to develop and provide a program for training parish volunteers who could visit and journey with parishioners facing life-threatening illnesses. These volunteers have truly been a gift to our parish and community, and to the lives of the parishioners and families they have touched.

Caring for those who are facing issues of death and dying is often referred to as end-of-life care, or hospice palliative care. In Ontario, Canada, where I live, our provincial palliative care association has a mission statement that captures the essence of what good end-of-life care encompasses.

> How we treat those who are dying in our community reflects who we are as a society. All Ontarians have the right to die with dignity, to have access to physical, psychosocial and spiritual care. As health care providers, volunteers, and family representatives of Ontario's hospice palliative care community we advocate for quality end-of-life care using an integrated and collaborative approach.[1]

Certainly, this approach reflects a holistic view and indicates the importance of addressing all needs, including the spiritual

needs of everyone involved in the circle of care. Having walked
with many people and their families as they faced the end of their
earthly life, I have witnessed some whose experience was beautiful and peaceful, and some who struggled deeply to the end,
seemingly filled with either denial, fear, angst, or a combination
of those. I wanted to be able to find a way to help people lessen,
or even overcome, not only their fear of dying but also their fear
of talking about it.

Many experts have written about various aspects of death and
dying over the years, but the book that truly inspired me was
authored by one of my favorite spiritual writers, Henri Nouwen.
In 1994, two years before his own sudden death, Henri published
a wonderful book titled *Our Greatest Gift: A Meditation on Dying and
Caring.* This book is filled with insights into how someone might
begin to explore the meaning of both one's life and one's death,
and how one's relationship with one's God and with others affects
both the way one lives and the way one dies.

> People are dying. Not just the few I know, but countless people
> everywhere, every day, every hour. Dying is the most general
> human event, something we all have to do. But do we do it well?
> Is our death more than an unavoidable fate that we simply wish
> would not be? Can it somehow become an act of fulfillment, per-
> haps more human than any other human act?[2]

Henri's words rang true to me. I began searching his writings,
and soon discovered a wealth of related stories and material in
many of his other works. My hope is that people will find the
teachings compiled in *Befriending Death* to be as accessible and as
valuable as I have.

Father Henri J. M. Nouwen was a Dutch, Roman Catholic priest,
as well as a psychologist. For many years he lived a life of privilege as a professor at Notre Dame and in the Divinity Schools of

Yale and Harvard. He taught and wrote extensively, being read by people of many faiths, including former First Lady Hillary Clinton, now Secretary of State. She has said that Henri's book *The Return of the Prodigal Son* helped her years ago during some of her darkest hours in the White House. "Nouwen's book contains universal, timeless lessons for people of all religions, backgrounds and cultures. . . . I would encourage everyone to read it, particularly if they are going through difficult times."[3]

Henri also spent time living with the poor in South America and living the life of a monk in a Trappist Monastery. Eventually he settled in Canada as pastor of a L'Arche community, living with people with disabilities. His life was profoundly changed by this community, and he penned many books about his experiences there.

Nouwen's knowledge about death and dying was gained by accompanying various family, friends, and community members as they journeyed through their own deaths, as well as experiencing a near-fatal traffic collision himself. Publishing more than forty books during his lifetime, he covered many spiritual topics including compassion, prayer, ministry, and community, and he wrote extensively about our identity as a beloved child of a loving God. However, in his later years, it was the theme of befriending our death which became the focus of his speaking and writing.

Certainly dying is one of the deep mysteries of our universal human experience. Henri's writings challenge us all to embrace this part of our life's journey with openness, inspiring us to move from fear to love. His belief was that all of us need to reflect on and befriend our death whether we are facing a life-threatening illness or not. As health care providers, ministers, or any others who journey with the dying, it is important for us to do this work and be comfortable speaking about death, so that we can enable those dying to do the same.

For me, this quest to answer my questions has been a true labor of love. I have learned so much and am indebted to many who assisted and inspired me. During my visits to the Henri J. M. Nouwen Archives and Research Collection at the University of St. Michael's College, John M. Kelly Library, in Toronto, and the extensive library at Cedars, I was introduced to a wealth of Henri's published and unpublished material. Through the hospitality extended to me during my stays at Daybreak, Henri's L'Arche community in Richmond Hill, I grew in my understanding of how he lived. I can better understand how he came to love those who loved him, and I thank all of them for sharing their lives and their stories with me.

Above all, I thank Henri for his willingness to be open and honest with his feelings and experiences, and for having the courage to share them with the world. His insights into how the Gospels are understood, and how God's Spirit is active in our lives, continue to be enlightening and refreshing. Throughout this project, and especially while staying at Cedars, the guest house at Daybreak and Henri's former home, I felt his spirit at work in my work. "Before his death, he told his friends that when he died his spirit would be accessible to those he loved and who loved him."[4]

This is not so much a "how-to" book, as one which is meant to inspire and prompt the reader to reflection and discussion. My prayer is that you will experience the essence of Henri Nouwen's spirituality in a deep and personal way, as you explore your own thoughts and beliefs about living and dying. As you begin, allow Henri to share some valuable wisdom which may give direction to your reading. "The inner life is always a life for others. When I myself am able to befriend death, I will be able to help others do the same."[5]

Chapter One

GETTING TO KNOW HENRI

For Henri Nouwen, 1932–1996, our generation's Kierkegaard. By sharing his own struggles, he mentored us all, helping us to pray while not knowing how to pray, to rest while feeling restless, to be at peace while tempted, to feel safe while still anxious, to be surrounded by a cloud of light while still in darkness, and to love while still in doubt.

dedication to *The Holy Longing*, by Ron Rolheiser

It has been said of Henri Nouwen, that he probably lived five or six lives in the space of one. It was not a particularly long life; he died suddenly at age 64. He pursued many varied interests, reached many people, wrote many books, lived very intensely, and accomplished much. He has also been referred to by many as one of the best-loved spiritual writers of our time. Michael O'Laughlin, who met Henri at Harvard and became his teaching assistant, forged a deep and lasting friendship with him. Michael has written extensively about Henri, and in his book titled *God's Beloved: A Spiritual Biography of Henri Nouwen,* he writes:

> The strange but undeniable truth about Henri Nouwen is that simply by being himself, he changed the way Christianity is practiced in the Western world. This may seem an impossibly large claim to make, putting Nouwen in the same category with persons such as C. S. Lewis in Britain, Billy Graham or Thomas Merton in the United

States. . . . Yet it is true: as modern Christians loosened up and became more personal, more humble, and more ecumenical, as Vatican II thinking took hold among Catholics, as we all refocused on Jesus and scripture, Henri Nouwen came to symbolize the important ways in which things were changing and where things were going.

Remarkably, he did this simply by holding fast to the heart of Christian experience, and by speaking frankly about his own doubts and limitations. . . . He wrote plainly and he spoke to the heart. What he created was an inspired vision of active and inquisitive faith, fashioned within his own brokenness and openness to God.[1]

Henri was born in the Netherlands, in the city of Nijkerk, on January 24, 1932, to Laurent and Maria Nouwen. His father was a professor of law at the Catholic University of Nijmegen, and his mother was religious as well as cultured, pursuing interests in literature and foreign languages. Her brother Anton was a priest, who later became an advisor to the Vatican on Jewish-Christian relations. He was certainly a strong role model for the young boy. Henri was the oldest of four children, and even though he was intelligent and a natural-born leader, he was restless, clumsy, and uncoordinated. Not one who excelled at sports, he gravitated toward religion, and by the age of five began speaking of the desire to be a priest. He had a very special bond with his mother, who was sensitive and thoughtful, and Henri reflected these characteristics in his personality as well. However, his relationship with his father was ambivalent. Laurent Nouwen was a man of enormous drive and intelligence, who placed a high value on competence, urging his boys to make something of themselves as he had done. Henri's insecurities were apparent early on and continued to permeate his adult life, as he felt that he could never measure up to his father's expectations.

In 1950, at age 18, Henri entered the minor seminary. During World War II, the Germans forced countless Catholic priests from occupied countries to work as laborers. Many, especially in France, desired to continue sharing in the life of the working people on a voluntary basis afterward. Theologians there experimented with new initiatives to engage the world and make sense of scientific advances and social change. Eventually the new ideas gained strength and spread to Belgium and Holland. Henri was involved by then with his uncle in ecumenical outreach to both Protestants and Jews, and was participating in new ways of being a Dutch Catholic. Innovative attitudes appeared and flourished, with an emerging Catholicism more open to the laity. The Church was attempting to speak to the needs of modern people in a changing world, trying to become more inclusive and attentive. "These were changes that Nouwen accepted and internalized. They would become hallmarks of the spirituality he would teach and promote for the rest of his life."2

Henri was ordained a priest in Utrecht, Holland, on July 21, 1957, by Archbishop Bernard Alfrink. The Catholic Church was heading into one of the greatest shifts in its history, and Holland would play a major role in the changes about to take place. Bishop Alfrink helped champion the reforms of the Second Vatican Council, also known as Vatican II.3

After his ordination in 1957, and with his bishop's permission, Henri went off to university at Nijmegen to study psychology. As a priest directly engaged in this "science of the mind," he struggled greatly with reconciling the divergent value systems of psychological theory and Catholicism. He eventually traveled to the United States where new programs were combining psychology and religion in a hybrid discipline called pastoral counseling. He met Gordon Allport, the famous psychologist, who taught at Harvard.

Allport advised Nouwen to finish his psychology studies in Nijmegen and thereafter to enroll in the program of studies in "religion and psychiatry" at the Menninger Institute in Topeka, Kansas.

He took Allport's advice, and from 1964 to 1966 Nouwen studied in Topeka. There he got to know many people who had ideas similar to his own. . . .

The Menninger Institute was the birthplace of pastoral psychology, and especially for the development of programs for clinical pastoral education (CPE).[4]

Henri's arrival in the United States in 1964 coincided with the third session of Vatican II.

As a Dutch priest who had been in Rome during conciliar sessions, Henri Nouwen was regarded in Kansas as a living representative of the new Catholicism among the Americans he met there. Although his primary focus continued to be the application of psychological theory to pastoral ministry, he quickly found a new role or "vocation" as a proponent of Vatican II spirituality in the United States.[5]

This period in Henri's life also saw a certain measure of political awakening. "The struggle of Martin Luther King, Jr., for Black civil rights brought the United States into a period of vehement protests. Nouwen participated in Martin Luther King's great march from Selma to Montgomery in 1965. This affected him deeply. . . . Little by little he came to know the American spiritual and political climate. He began to feel at home here."[6] However, his intention at the time was not to stay in the United States but to eventually return to the Netherlands to teach.

In the meantime, a friend from the Menninger Institute asked Henri to come to the University of Notre Dame and teach in a new department of psychology. He did so from 1966 to 1968, developing classes in pastoral psychology. "Those classes became the basis of a number of articles that were compiled in the book *Intimacy*. It was Nouwen's first book and the beginning of a long series of publications."[7]

Nouwen returned to the Netherlands briefly, both to teach and to study, having been granted a Doctorandus degree in psychology. He felt like somewhat of a failure that the Doctorate degree eluded him, when his dissertation topic was rejected on the grounds that it lacked a statistical base and theological depth. It was during this bleak time in his life, when he was filled with loneliness and frustration, that he began some of his most significant writing. "He wrote in isolation, yet nevertheless began to produce the books of theological and spiritual reflection that would ultimately become his greatest gift to the church and the world. He was not well received in Holland, but this new style of writing was resonating with publishers and readers in America, a land that had apparently not forgotten him."[8]

He was eventually approached by the Divinity School at Yale, and decided to return to the United States to teach. As a European diocesan priest working in a university that was both Protestant and American, he was comfortably able to take Catholic ecumenical advances to new levels, and he began to impart and exemplify a new type of Christianity that could be embraced by all Christian churches. His years at Yale, 1971 to 1981, were fruitful ones. He wrote thirteen books during that time. *Reaching Out: The Three Movements of the Spiritual Life*, published in 1975, has become a spiritual classic.

> This book is a response to the question: "What does it mean to live a life in the Spirit of Jesus Christ?" Therefore, it is a personal book, a book born out of struggles which in the first place were and still are my own. But during the years it became more and more clear that by deepening these struggles, by following them to their roots, I was touching a level where they could be shared. This book does not offer answers or solutions but is written in the conviction that the quest for an authentic Christian spirituality is worth the effort and the pain, since in the midst of this quest we can find signs offering hope, courage and confidence.[9]

Henri's popularity as a professor was becoming matched by his growing reputation as a spiritual writer. He taught classes on ministry to the elderly and prisoners, on discipleship, on prayer, on the relationship of spirituality and ministry, on ministry in secular institutions, and even on the ministry of Vincent van Gogh and Thomas Merton. He was becoming more widely read and quoted as an authority in the field of pastoral ministry and spirituality.

Henri Nouwen ended up spending more time with students than any other faculty member, and he made friendships with dozens of them that would last for decades. As students began to arrive at Yale specifically because of Nouwen's presence there, some of the faculty did become somewhat envious. . . . [W]hile they toiled in the library to produce serious works of scholarship, he dashed off little books on spiritual themes that anyone might read and enjoy. They were serious scholars, but he was the popular one whom everyone was reading.[10]

Someone who greatly influenced Henri's spirituality and writing at this time was Thomas Merton, a Trappist monk, who was also an innovator and gifted writer. Nouwen met and talked with Merton on a visit to his Kentucky monastery, regarding him as an extremely valuable guide in looking at how to address modern society from a spiritual perspective. "Merton was to solidify for Nouwen the conviction that a life of prayer should ideally center on a kind of contemplation that took the world in, understood it, and saw in it the coming of Jesus. . . . In ways small and large Nouwen absorbed the teachings of Merton and made them his own."[11]

Over the years, psychology, as a framework for Henri, was being replaced by creativity, contemplation, and engagement in the spiritual life.

In 1974, the same year that he received tenure at Yale, he took a seven-month sabbatical as a "temporary" resident with the

Trappist monks at the Abbey of the Genesee in upstate New York. A daily journal of prayerful reflections and conversations with spiritual director Dom John Eudes Bamberger resulted in his best-selling book *Genesee Diary* (1976). After Henri's mother died in October 1978, he would return to the abbey for another six months. . . . Throughout his adult life, Henri was caught up in a cycle of long, hectic days of teaching and service, followed by periods of nervous exhaustion, depression, and insomnia. In part, his visits to the Genesee Abbey were motivated by a desire to break this cycle.[12]

However, Henri's friend Robert Jonas goes on to tell us why Henri never excelled in the monastic lifestyle.

Henri's vision of a warm and regular monastic life foundered on the rocks of his predisposition to restlessness, the desire for fresh intellectual stimulation, a hunger for new friends and experiences, and a nagging, sometimes self-defeating inability to say no. All too often the friends who initially supported his periods of rest suddenly needed him for counseling, weddings, funerals, and lectures. His familiar response, "Yes, of course," was partly motivated by his desire to live his life for others, just as Jesus had done. I, and perhaps thousands of others, are thankful that Henri was so motivated. But there were probably other, more unconscious motivations as well, such as the habitual, almost neurotic need to be needed. For all of Henri's life, each of his sabbaticals and retreats would be interrupted by several quick taxi rides to bustling airports, to quiet death-bed scenes, or to rooms filled with hundreds of people who waited eagerly for a word of hope and inspiration. And Henri knew himself well. He knew that often he himself could not follow his own advice, to stay home and pray.[13]

The 1970s in Latin America was a time of turmoil and of the birth of liberation theology. Henri made friends with priests and lay missionaries there, traveling to Bolivia in the summer of 1972 to study Spanish. He returned after resigning from Yale in 1981, staying until March of 1982. The diary he kept during that stay was later published under the title *¡Gracias!*, followed by *Love in a Fearful Land: A Guatemalan Story*. Though he loved the people in Latin America and learned much from them, he did not feel called to the life of a missionary. "If I have any vocation in Latin America, it is the vocation to receive from the people the gifts they have to offer us and to bring these gifts back up north for our own conversion and healing."[14]

In 1983 he attempted teaching again and signed a contract with Harvard Divinity School as a Professor of Divinity. Between first and second semester, he traveled to Trosly, France, to visit a L'Arche community established by Jean Vanier. A L'Arche community is a special place where people with developmental and/or physical handicaps live in community with their caregivers. These disabled, or "differently-abled," persons are called "core members" because they are at the heart of the community life that forms around them. "[T]he community for the handicapped is called L'Arche, a constant reminder of Noah's Ark, to which people and animals fled for shelter as the flood covered more and more of the land. L'Arche is indeed the place where many vulnerable men and women who are threatened by the judgemental and violent world in which they live can find a safe place and feel at home."[15] Michael O'Laughlin gives us the history of this community and the L'Arche movement itself.

> Jean Vanier is a Swiss-born Canadian and the son of the very distinguished Georges Vanier, the former governor general of Canada. Georges and his wife Pauline led such exemplary lives of service and Christian witness, particularly during and after World War II, when they offered great assistance to refugees, that they are now being considered for beatification by the Catholic Church.
>
> After obtaining a doctorate in philosophy in Paris, their son Jean taught in Toronto, then abandoned academia and joined his

spiritual director, Père Thomas Philippe, in Trosly. There he set up a residence in a small house. To this residence he brought two mentally handicapped men from a nearby institution where Père Thomas worked in order to live in long-term solidarity with them. He called the foyer he established L'Arche, which is French for "the ark." Soon other handicapped men and women arrived, as did young volunteers who agreed to live with and assist them for a year or more.

Thus, from a small gesture of hospitality and solidarity was born an international movement that now numbers more than one hundred communities around the world. L'Arche is set up as an ecumenical community, but the sensitive spirituality of French Catholicism is a very strong component of the Trosly community. From its French origins comes its sacramentality, a slower pace, an attention to small details and humble people, and a readiness to turn every meal and gathering into a celebration.[16]

Henri returned to Harvard, and in December 1984, he visited Trosly again, this time staying for a thirty-day retreat. Soon Nouwen realized he no longer felt at home at Harvard. "The environment of this world-famous university with all its constraints and pressures seemed completely opposed to what he had discovered in Latin America and even more at Trosly: life with the poor. The words that he used to typify the vast distance between the two ways of life are 'upward mobility' and 'downward mobility'."[17] Nouwen left Harvard at the end of that semester, and, after teaching a summer course at Boston College, proceeded to France for a twelve-month stay at L'Arche that would change his life forever.

In October 1985, Nouwen made a ten-day visit to the L'Arche community "Daybreak" in Richmond Hill, a suburb of Toronto, Canada. While he was there, one of the core members, Raymond, was struck by a car and critically injured. Henri stepped forward to provide pastoral support to the community and to Raymond's family. "In my nine days at Daybreak I came to feel intimately a

part of the intense joys and sorrows of this community of care. I
have a deep love for the handicapped men and women and their
assistants, who all received me with such warm hospitality. They
did not hide anything from me. They allowed me to see their fears
and their love."[18] Later in December, the Daybreak community
sent a letter to Henri asking him to consider returning to live with
them as their pastor. In *The Road to Daybreak*, he explains the
impact this invitation had on him.

> Joe writes, "This letter comes to you from the Daybreak
> Community Council and we are asking you to consider coming to
> live with us in our community of Daybreak. . . . We truly feel that
> you have a gift to bring us. At the same time, our sense is that
> Daybreak would be a good place for you, too. We would want to
> support you in your important vocation of writing and speaking by
> providing you with a home and with a community that will love
> you and call you to grow."
>
> I am deeply moved by this letter. It is the first time in my life
> that I have been explicitly called. All my work as a priest since my
> ordination has been a result of my own initiative. My work at the
> Menninger Clinic, Notre Dame, Yale, and Harvard and in Latin
> America has been work that I myself chose. . . .
>
> But now a community is saying, "We call you to live with us;
> to give to us and receive from us." I know that Joe's invitation is
> not a job offer but a genuine call to come and live with the poor.
> They have no money to offer, no attractive living quarters, no pres-
> tige. This is a completely new thing. It is a concrete call to follow
> Christ, to leave the world of success, accomplishment, and honor,
> and to trust Jesus and him alone.[19]

And so, at the end of August 1986, Henri Nouwen moved to
Daybreak. It would become his new, and final, home. Over the
next ten years, he would experience, perhaps, the greatest chapter of his life. However, in order to understand how Henri came

to reflect and write more intently on death and dying, it is necessary to consider some of the major turning points and events in his life.

THE DEATH OF MARIA NOUWEN

There were many events throughout Henri's life, prior to moving to Daybreak, which shaped his thinking, his writing, and his spirituality. Certainly his childhood, his ordination, his deep friendships and relationships, his years of learning and teaching in some of the most prestigious universities in the world, all affected his growth and life. However, one significant event, which certainly caused him to look more deeply at death and dying, was his beloved mother's sudden illness and death in 1978.

While Henri was teaching at Yale, his parents came to the United States to visit him. During their visit, his mother became gravely ill, and on her return to Holland was diagnosed with cancer. She only lived a few days after having surgery, and Henri rushed to Holland to be with his family and his dying mother. They shared a very close relationship; his mother had often given him emotional support and been his confidante throughout his life. Her death was a terrible blow to him, and he processed the experience by sharing his reflections in a small book titled *In Memoriam*.

My mother died. This event cannot claim any uniqueness. It is among the most common of human experiences. . . . Still, I want to reflect on this event because, although it is not unusual, exceptional or extraordinary, it remains in many ways unknown and unfathomed. It is indeed in the usual, normal and ordinary events that we touch the mystery of human life. When a child is born, a man and woman embrace, or a mother or father dies, the mystery of life reveals itself to us. It is precisely in the moments when we are most human, most in touch with what binds us together, that we discover the hidden depths of life. This is the reason why I feel free now to speak about my mother, whom I have loved so dearly and whose death is causing me such deep grief. In many different ways she has told me, and still tells me, that what is most universal is also most personal.

. . . Now she is no longer just my mother; she is a woman whose son wants to speak about what she has revealed to him, not only in her life but also in her death. In life she belonged to a few, in death she is for all.[20]

Weeks later, as Henri continued to process his grief and emotions, he wrote:

To remember her does not mean telling her story over and over again to my friends, nor does it mean pictures on the wall or a stone on her grave; it does not even mean constantly thinking about her. No. It means making her a participant in God's ongoing work of redemption by allowing her to dispel in me a little more of my darkness and lead me a little closer to the light. In these weeks of mourning she died in me more and more every day, making it impossible for me to cling to her as my mother. Yet by letting her go I did not lose her. Rather, I found that she is closer to me than ever. In and through the Spirit of Christ, she indeed is becoming a part of my very being.[21]

"I began to realize that she would never abandon us. That deep sense of safety she had given to us, that feeling of belonging to a world which could be trusted, would not die with her but would anchor itself more deeply in our being."[22] Six months later, Henri wrote a long letter of consolation to his father, which was eventually published. "Ever since we saw her still face in the hospital, we have wondered what death really is. It is a question mother has left us with, and we want to face it, enter it, explore it, and let it grow in us. By so doing we may be able to console one another."[23]

After Henri moved to Daybreak in 1986, there were many lessons learned, stories told, and many more books written. In fact, twenty-eight books and countless articles were penned between his arrival there and his untimely and sudden death in 1996. Many more have been published since then, either about him or his own material compiled by others. Although there were countless instances of growth and learning for him during the ten years at Daybreak, three important things happened which would greatly affect his life and his writings—especially his reflections on living and dying.

LIVING WITH ADAM

The first life-changing experience for Henri on arriving at Daybreak was moving into a basement bedroom in the New House, one of the eight homes in the community, and learning to live with housemates. "I was told that L'Arche's mission was to 'live with' core members, so I embarked on my new life. . . . Manual work, cooking, and housekeeping skills were alien to me. I had been teaching for twenty years, . . . and during this time I had never given much attention to creating a home nor had I been close to people with disabilities."[24] Henri was soon asked to assist core member Adam Arnett with his morning routine. This was terrifying to him, since he had never cared for anyone before, let alone someone with immense needs, who could not communicate, and who had frequent epileptic seizures.

At first I had to keep asking myself and others, "Why have you asked me to do this? Why did I say yes? What am I doing here? Who is this stranger who is demanding such a big chunk of my time each day? Why should I, the least capable of all the people in the house, be asked to take care of Adam and not of someone whose needs are a bit less?" The answer was always the same: "So you can get to know Adam."[25]

Gradually, Henri became more relaxed and confident in caring for Adam, and began to really get to know him. Adam became a confidant for Henri, who listened while Henri spoke to him about many things during their morning hours together. Although Adam could not speak, Henri grew to know him and love him and understand him deeply.

As I grew closer to Adam, I came to experience his most beautiful heart as the gateway to his real self, to his person, his soul, and his spirit. His heart, so transparent, reflected for me not only his person but also the heart of the universe and, indeed, the heart of God. After my many years of studying, reflecting, and teaching theology, Adam came into my life, and by his life and his heart he announced to me and summarized all I had ever learned.[26]

From September 1995 to September 1996, Henri was on a sabbatical from being pastor of Daybreak in order to rest, travel, and write. During that time, Adam's health deteriorated, and he died on February 12, 1996. Henri had traveled back to Richmond Hill to be with Adam and his family, and reflects on the moments at Adam's bedside after his death.

I couldn't stop gazing at his face. I thought, "Here is the man who more than anyone connected me with my inner self, my community, and my God. Here is the man I was asked to care for, but who took me into his life and into his heart in such an incredibly deep way. Yes, I had cared for him during my first year at Daybreak and had come to love him so much, but he has been such an invaluable gift to me. Here is my counselor, my teacher, and my guide, who could never say a word to me but taught me more than any book, professor, or spiritual director. Here is Adam, my friend, my beloved friend, the most vulnerable person I have ever known and at the same time the most powerful. He is dead now. His life is over. His task is accomplished. He has returned to the heart of God from which he came.[27]

After Adam's death, Henri began to write about their relationship, and the effect Adam's friendship had on him. Ironically, Henri died suddenly seven months later. Sue Mosteller, Henri's dear friend, took the unfinished manuscript and completed the book, titled *Adam: God's Beloved*, publishing it in 1997. Sue writes in the foreword:

> What struck me initially was the power and the significance of this relationship between Adam and Henri. It happened at a particular moment in Henri's life when he was searching for home. Adam, by his simplicity and by his presence, welcomed Henri home. It is an incredible story. . . .
>
> Henri patterns Adam's story after the life of Jesus, and he does it beautifully. Not only that, but he realized in the writing that Adam's story is his own story. Finally, by his genius as a writer, Henri gifts each of us with our stories as well.[28]

HENRI'S PLUNGE INTO DARKNESS

A year or so after arriving at Daybreak, a second life-changing event occurred: Henri experienced a profound psychological and emotional crisis. *The Inner Voice of Love: A Journey through Anguish to Freedom*, is one of Henri's most well known and well read books. Perhaps this is because so many people from all walks of life can relate to his pain and anguish, his depression and loss of hope. The book was published many years after his breakdown, from the diary he kept during that time. No one describes the events surrounding this time better than Henri himself, who shares his insights with the reader in the Introduction.

> This book is my secret journal. It was written during the most difficult period of my life, from December 1987 to June 1988. That was a time of extreme anguish, during which I wondered whether I

would be able to hold on to my life. Everything came crashing down—my self-esteem, my energy to live and work, my sense of being loved, my hope for healing, my trust in God . . . everything. Here I was, a writer about the spiritual life, known as someone who loves God and gives hope to people, flat on the ground and in total darkness.

What happened? I had come face to face with my own nothingness. It was as if all that had given my life meaning was pulled away and I could see nothing in front of me but a bottomless abyss.

The strange thing was that this happened shortly after I had found my true home. After many years of life in universities, where I never felt fully at home, I had become a member of L'Arche, a community of men and women with mental disabilities. I had been received with open arms, given all the attention and affection I could ever hope for, and offered a safe place to hit bottom!

Just when all those around me were assuring me they loved me, cared for me, appreciated me, yes, even admired me, I experienced myself as a useless, unloved, and despicable person. Just when people were putting their arms around me, I saw the endless depth of my human misery and felt that there was nothing worth living for. Just when I had found a home, I felt absolutely homeless. Just when I was being praised for my spiritual insights, I felt devoid of faith. Just when people were thanking me for bringing them closer to God, I felt that God had abandoned me. It was as if the house I had finally found had no floors. The anguish completely paralyzed me. . . .

All of this was triggered by the sudden interruption of a friendship. Going to L'Arche and living with very vulnerable people, I had gradually let go of many of my inner guards and opened my heart more fully to others. Among my many friends, one had been able to touch me in a way I had never been touched before. Our friendship encouraged me to allow myself to be loved and cared for with greater trust and confidence. It was a totally new experience for me, and it brought immense joy and peace. It seemed as if a door of my interior life had been opened, a door that had remained locked during my youth and most of my adult life.

But this deeply satisfying friendship became the road to my anguish, because soon I discovered that the enormous space that had been opened for me could not be filled by the one who had opened it. I became possessive, needy, and dependent, and when the friendship finally had to be interrupted, I fell apart. I felt abandoned, rejected, and betrayed. . . .

Intellectually I knew that no human friendship could fulfill the deepest longing of my heart. I knew that only God could give me what I desired. I knew that I had been set on a road where nobody could walk with me but Jesus. But all this knowledge didn't help me in my pain.[29]

Henri realized he needed to leave the community for a time, and he chose a center where he could be treated for his deep depression. He found a place where he could be given the psychological and spiritual attention that he needed so that he could address the issues which had surfaced. "To my surprise, I never lost the ability to write. In fact, writing became part of my struggle for survival. . . . When I returned to my community, I reread all I had written during the time of my 'exile.' It seemed so intense and raw that I could hardly imagine it would speak to anyone but me."[30]

Very old places of pain that had been hidden to me were opened up, and fearful experiences from my early years were brought to consciousness. The interruption of friendship forced me to enter the basement of my soul and look directly at what was hidden there, to choose, in the face of it all, not death but life. Thanks to my attentive and caring guides, I was able day by day to take very small steps toward life. I could easily have become bitter, resentful, depressed, and suicidal. That this did not happen was the result of the struggle expressed in this book.[31]

Eight years later, many friends of Henri encouraged him to publish parts of his diary, so that others could be nurtured by the spiritual insights gained during this time in his life. The writings show that light and darkness, hope and despair, love and fear are never very far from each other. Often, one finds that spiritual freedom requires a fierce spiritual battle such as this. In the end, Henri published the writings, and was also able to ultimately restore the friendship.

HENRI'S BRUSH WITH DEATH

A third life-changing event in Henri's life during his time at Daybreak came in 1989, when he was involved in a near-fatal accident with a van. One icy morning, Henri left to walk down the side of the highway to one of the L'Arche homes where he was to care for a core member named Hsi-Fu. In the cold darkness, he was struck by the mirror of a passing van and thrown onto the pavement. After arriving at the hospital, it was determined that he had extensive internal bleeding and would have to have emergency surgery to remove his injured spleen. "Faced with the possibility of dying, it came to me that the mirror of the passing van had forced me to look at myself in a radically new way."[32]

> Somewhere, deep in me, I sensed that my life was in real danger. And so I let myself enter into a place I had never been before: the portal of death. I wanted to know that place, to "walk around" it, and make myself ready for a life beyond life. It was the first time in my life that I consciously walked into this seemingly fearful place, the first time I looked forward to what might be a new way of being. I tried to let go of my familiar world, my history, my friends, my plans. I tried not to look back, but ahead. I kept looking at that door that might open to me and show me something beyond anything I had ever seen.
>
> What I experienced then was something I had never experi-

enced before: pure and unconditional love. Better still, what I experienced was an intensely personal presence, a presence that pushed all my fears aside and said, "Come, don't be afraid. I love you." . . . It was not a warm light, a rainbow, or an open door that I saw, but a human yet divine presence that I felt, inviting me to come closer and to let go of all fears. My whole life had been an arduous attempt to follow Jesus as I had come to know him through my parents, friends, and teachers. I had spent countless hours studying the Scriptures, listening to lectures and sermons, and reading spiritual books. Jesus had been very close to me, but also very distant; a friend, but also a stranger; a source of hope, but also of fear, guilt, and shame. But now, when I walked around the portal of death, all ambiguity and all uncertainty were gone. He was there, the Lord of my life, saying, "Come to me, come."

. . . This experience was the realization of my oldest and deepest desires. Since the first moment of consciousness, I have had the desire to be with Jesus. Now I felt his presence in a most tangible way, as if my whole life had come together and I was being enfolded in love.[33]

Henri captured the story, along with his feelings and experiences, in a book titled *Beyond the Mirror.* In the prologue, he explains his intent in sharing it.

I have written it because I had no choice. My accident brought me to the portal of death and led me to a new experience of God. Not writing about it would have been unfaithful to my vocation to proclaim the presence of God at all times and in all places. Books and articles have been important in my search for God, but it has been the interruptions to my everyday life that have most revealed to me the divine mystery of which I am a part.[34]

This near-death encounter was another turning point in his life's journey, which led Henri to continue his search to understand more about death and dying. It was followed by a personal search to reflect on his own dying and to write about it. Henri eventually spent five weeks in solitude at a friend's apartment in Germany to ponder and write about his own mortality. The product was *Our Greatest Gift: A Meditation on Dying and Caring*, a wonderful book which was the inspiration for my own book.

Then in 1995, after nine years at Daybreak, Henri embarked on a one-year sabbatical. The community sent him off with a mandate to say no to all work except writing. He also promised himself that he would not let a day pass without writing down the things that were happening within and around him. During that time, he traveled extensively, wrote four books, and returned to Daybreak on August 30, 1996, after making his last entry in the nearly seven-hundred-page diary of what would be his final year. However, before he could settle down again in Canada, he had one last project to attend to.

Years before, while he was still teaching at Harvard, he had been introduced to a poster of Rembrandt's famous painting of the Prodigal Son and was immediately drawn to its beauty. Three years later, before he left France to move to Daybreak, he had the opportunity to visit the Soviet Union and sit before the actual painting in the Hermitage in Saint Petersburg. He wrote one of his most famous spiritual books, *The Return of the Prodigal Son*, after that visit. Now, in September of 1996, plans had been made for him to do a film for Dutch television on the theme of the Prodigal Son and on Rembrandt's painting, shooting part of it in Russia.

Henri flew to Holland, met with the film crew, and checked into his hotel. He fell extremely ill and was rushed to hospital, where it was determined he had had a heart attack. Word went out quickly to family in Europe and friends in Canada, and soon many were at his side. Over the next number of days, he rallied, and seemed to be out of immediate danger. However, he suffered another series of heart attacks and died alone on September 21, 1996, at the age of 64.

HIS PURPOSE

Henri reflected at different times during his life on what he thought his mission and purpose was. As he grew, changed, and experienced some of the profound life-altering situations alluded to above, his articulation of that mission became more focused and succinct. *Sabbatical Journey,* the book published from the diary of his final year, contains many entries which speak to his reflections on this topic. This passage reveals for us how deep his own convictions about faith and salvation were, and yet, how in embracing the whole of humanity as he believed God did, he could make some sense of a more global perspective.

> My conviction as a young man was that there is no salvation outside the Catholic Church and that it was my task to bring all "nonbelievers" into the one true church.
>
> But much has happened to me over the years. My own psychological training, my exposure to people from the most different religious backgrounds, the Second Vatican Council, the new theology of mission, and my life in L'Arche have all deepened and broadened my views on Jesus' saving work. Today I personally believe that while Jesus came to open the door to God's house, all human beings can walk through that door, whether they know about Jesus or not. Today I see it as my call to help every person claim his or her own way to God. I feel deeply called to witness for Jesus as the one who is the source of my own spiritual journey and thus create the possibility for other people to know Jesus and commit themselves to him. I am so truly convinced that the Spirit of God is present in our midst and that each person can be touched by God's Spirit in ways far beyond my own comprehension and intention.[35]

In another entry he writes, "One thing is clearer to me than ever: What I think, say, and do makes a difference. . . . More than ever I realize that I have to keep writing and thus serving the truth in simplicity, honesty, and humility."[36] When asked by a friend what was most important in his life, Henri responded, "Well, three things: living a vision inspired by the Gospel of Jesus; being close to the poor, the handicapped, the sick, and the dying; and finding a way to satisfy my deep yearning for intimacy and affection."[37]

In both *Our Greatest Gift* and *Beyond the Mirror* Nouwen explains why he is so compelled to write about the topic of death and dying.

> I want to believe that beyond the fatal battle for survival is a hopeful battle for life. I want to believe—indeed, I do believe—that, ultimately, love is stronger than death. I have no argument to present. I have only the story of Jesus and the stories of those who trust in the life-giving truth of his life and his word. These stories show me a new way of living and a new way of dying, and I have a profound desire to show that way to others.[38]

> Somehow I believed that writing was one way to let something of lasting value emerge from the pains and fears of my little, quickly passing life. Each time life required me to take a new step into unknown spiritual territory, I felt a deep, inner urge to tell my story to others—perhaps as a need for companionship but maybe, too, out of an awareness that my deepest vocation is to be a witness to the glimpses of God I have been allowed to catch.[39]

In reflecting on his brush with death and his return to "this side" of eternal life, Nouwen writes:

> [H]aving had a glimpse beyond the mirror of life, I now wonder if our eagerness to hold on to this life does not suggest that we have lost contact with one of the most essential aspects of our creed: the faith in eternal life.
> . . . Theology means looking at the world from God's perspective. Perhaps I am given an opportunity to live more theologically

and to help others to do the same without their having to be hit by
the mirror of a passing van.[40]

"It is the way of witness. I must remain on the other side while
being sent back. I have to live eternity while exploring the human
search in time. I have to belong to God while giving myself to
people."[41] This seems to be the dilemma which we all face in our
lives—knowing in the depths of our hearts that we truly "belong"
to God, while we give ourselves to others. Henri, indeed, spent a
lifetime trying to understand that and live it himself, while feeling
called to share it through his living and his writing for others.
Deirdre LaNoue captures the essence of Henri's life and ministry
in this reflection about his death, from *The Spiritual Legacy of Henri
Nouwen.*

At the death of Henri Nouwen, Americans, as well as the rest of the
world, lost a significant spiritual guide. His loss is deeply felt by
those who knew him and those who read him. Nouwen was not
perfect. His transparency concerning his own struggles could make
a person uncomfortable at times. But the value of a guide is found
in his or her ability to meet you where you are, to understand how
you got there, and to lead you to where you need to be. Nouwen
was a spiritual guide who was well acquainted with the struggle of
the spiritual journey but he had also glimpsed the hope of living in
the light of God's love. Inasmuch as he longed deeply to know the
love of God for himself, he longed for others to know this surpass-
ing love as well. He spent the majority of his life trying to point the
way and he continues to do so through his writings. This is Henri
Nouwen's spiritual legacy.[42]

Chapter Two

HALLMARKS OF NOUWEN'S SPIRITUALITY

Sue Mosteller, one of Henri's closest friends, shares her thoughts on Henri's spirituality in this excerpt from her eulogy given at his funeral in Toronto.

> We have only to look around this church to see the ways in which he built bridges between us and brought us together: rich and poor, from north and south, from family in Holland to family in Canada, from differing backgrounds, cultures, and religious denominations. Henri brought us together. . . . *Now he has left us and it is the time for us to take responsibility for the spirituality he gave us.* If we enter into the privileged and very sacred center of our hearts and listen to God's Spirit who is living there, we will hear the message that Henri was sent to teach us: Don't be afraid of your pain, choose to love when relationships are difficult, choose to believe when hope is flagging, help each other, step through wounded and bitter feelings to be in union with one another, forgive each other from your hearts because God is near, calling each one of us, "Beloved." This call to step out of our spiritual adolescence is Henri's legacy.[1] (Emphasis mine.)

How do we begin to understand this "spirituality that he gave us," especially as it pertains to befriending death and dying well? Trying to define the word "spirituality" is difficult, and there are as many definitions as there are authors who are writing about it.

Bookstores today, both church and secular alike, literally teem with books on spirituality. Elizabeth Dreyer, in her article on Christian spirituality in the *HarperCollins Encyclopedia of Catholicism*, distinguishes Christian spirituality from other types:

> Christian spirituality is the daily, communal, lived expression of one's ultimate beliefs characterized by openness to the self-transcending love of God, self, neighbor, and world through Jesus Christ and in the power of the Spirit.[2]

Henri Nouwen's view of Christian spirituality is in harmony with this, since he addresses these key themes in his writings: how to nurture one's relationship with God, with self, and with others through the love of Jesus and the power of the Holy Spirit.

Nouwen's books were often born out of his own psychological and spiritual journey. His training in psychology and spirituality allowed him to reframe concepts into language that any person of any faith background or education could understand and use in his or her own life. His easy way of relating to people from every walk of life and his deep humility and brutal honesty about his own fears and struggles were a large part of what made him such a beloved author and spiritual guide during his lifetime. This legacy continues as strong as ever today.

Although Henri taught, spoke, and wrote extensively, covering a wide range of topics, there were a few golden threads woven through many of his writings. In order to examine what he has written about befriending death, it will be helpful to have some insight into some of Nouwen's basic spiritual beliefs and understandings.

THE HEART OF GOD

Who is God? How do we come to know about God? How do we find God? Nouwen's deeply personal meditation on

Luke's Gospel about the wayward son changed his life and what he understood about how God loved him. Nouwen spent hours actually sitting in front of Rembrandt's painting *The Return of the Prodigal Son,* taking in the subtle artistic nuances which brought the narrative to life. This helped him begin to grasp the story more completely and to discover the kind of love available to him from a Father who reached out to him personally.

> When I saw the Rembrandt poster for the first time in the fall of 1983, all my attention was drawn to the hands of the old father pressing his returning boy to his chest. I saw forgiveness, reconciliation, healing; I also saw safety, rest, being at home. I was so deeply touched by this image of the life-giving embrace of father and son because everything in me yearned to be received in the way the prodigal son was received. That encounter turned out to be the beginning of my own return.[3]

Further reflection on the hands of Rembrandt's father led Nouwen not only to a new understanding of how God loved him but also to an expanded and radically different image of who God was for him.

> It all began with the hands. The two are quite different. The father's left hand touching the son's shoulder is strong and muscular. . . .
> How different is the father's right hand! This hand does not hold or grasp. It is refined, soft, and very tender. The fingers are close to each other and they have an elegant quality. It lies gently upon the son's shoulder. It wants to caress, to stroke, and to offer consolation and comfort. It is a mother's hand. . . .
> As soon as I recognized the difference between the two hands of the father, a new world of meaning opened up for me. The father is not simply a great patriarch. He is mother as well as father. He touches the son with a masculine hand and a feminine hand.

He holds, and she caresses. He confirms and she consoles. He is, indeed, God, in whom manhood and womanhood, fatherhood and motherhood, are fully present.[4]

In spiritual writing and understanding today, we continue to seek language which expresses more completely the images of a God who is not male or female but who encompasses all characteristics of a loving creator and parent, as Henri discovered. Readers of Nouwen's books will find that in his later years he was more aware of using inclusive God-language. Sue Mosteller explained to me that Henri was beginning to understand how important this was in his writing, but found the Prodigal Son too challenging to change because of all of the male figures in the story. Today, as revisions are made in new editions of his books, the Henri Nouwen Legacy Trust and Henri Nouwen Society are trying to be more aware of using inclusive language, believing that Henri himself would believe that to be important.

Through his encounter with the painting and the story, Nouwen also discovered new understandings about the heart of God, and how God loves.

There is no doubt—in the parable or the painting—about the father's heart. His heart goes out to both of his sons; he loves them both; . . .

As I let all of this sink in, I see how the story of the father and his lost sons powerfully affirms that it was not I who chose God, but God who first chose me. This is the great mystery of our faith. We do not choose God, God chooses us. From all eternity we are hidden "in the shadow of God's hand" and "engraved on his palm." Before any human touches us, God "forms us in secret" . . . "knits us together in our mother's womb." God loves us before any human person can show love to us. He loves us with a "first" love, an unlimited, unconditional love, wants us to be his beloved children, and tells us to become as loving as himself.[5]

Henri reflects more deeply on this concept, realizing for perhaps the first time that he does not take the initiative in this relationship.

For most of my life I have struggled to find God, to know God, to love God. I have tried hard to follow the guidelines of the spiritual life—pray always, work for others, read the Scriptures—and to avoid the many temptations to dissipate myself. I have failed many times but always tried again, even when I was close to despair.

Now I wonder whether I have sufficiently realized that during all this time God has been trying to find me, to know me, and to love me. The question is not "How am I to find God?" but "How am I to let myself be found by him?" The question is not "How am I to know God?" but "How am I to let myself be known by God?" And, finally, the question is not "How am I to love God?" but "How am I to let myself be loved by God?" God is looking into the distance for me, trying to find me, and longing to bring me home. . . .

It might sound strange, but God wants to find me as much as, if not more than, I want to find God. Yes, God needs me as much as I need God. God is not the patriarch who stays home, doesn't move, and expects his children to come to him, apologize for their aberrant behavior, beg for forgiveness, and promise to do better. To the contrary, he leaves the house, ignoring his dignity by running toward them, pays no heed to apologies and promises of change, and brings them to the table richly prepared for them.[6]

Once Henri realizes this for himself, he sees it as his mission to share this insight with others. He is truly grateful for having discovered this in his own life, and desires for all people to understand these things about our God of love. "So we have known and believe the love that God has for us. God is love, and those who abide in love abide in God, and God abides in them. We love because he first loved us" (1 Jn 4:16, 19 NRSV).

Here lies hidden the great call to conversion: to look . . . with the eyes of God's love. . . . . [I]f I am able to look at the world with the eyes of God's love and discover that God's vision is not that of a stereotypical landowner or patriarch but rather that of an all-giving and forgiving father who does not measure out his love to his children according to how well they behave, then I quickly see that my only true response can be deep gratitude.[7]

Deirdre LaNoue, in her book *The Spiritual Legacy of Henri Nouwen*, comments on Nouwen's beliefs about God's love, followed by Nouwen's own words on the subject (in italics).

The other side of the paradox in the struggle to love God alone was Nouwen's belief that "we cannot find God. We can only be found by him." In other words, the challenge of a spiritual relationship with God was not figuring out how to initiate a relationship with God, but learning how to respond to the relationship that God himself had already initiated in love through Jesus. This changed the focus from how much Nouwen loved God to how much God loved him, and Nouwen had a great deal to say about the unconditional love of God.[8]

What can we say about God's love? We can say that God's love is unconditional. God does not say, "I love you, if . . . ." There are no ifs in God's heart. God's love for us does not depend on what we do or say, on our looks or intelligence, on our success or popularity. God's love for us existed before we were born and will exist after we have died. God's love is from eternity to eternity and is not bound to any time-related events or circumstances. Does that mean that God does not care what we do or say? No, because God's love wouldn't be real if God didn't care. To love without condition does not mean to love without concern. God desires to enter into relationship with us and wants us to love God in return.

> *Let's dare to enter into an intimate relationship with God*
> *without fear, trusting that we will receive love and always more*
> *love.*[9]

"The most important thing you can say about God's love is that God loves us not because of anything we've done to earn that love, but because God, in total freedom, has decided to love us."[10] "Let's pray that we can let go of our fear of God and embrace God as the source of all love."[11]

Clearly, much of what Nouwen came to know about God was rooted in what he learned from the life of Jesus as found in the Gospels.

> Although Nouwen speaks often of God, it is the person of Jesus, God incarnate, who most clearly reveals God the Father and demonstrates how to be in relationship with him. . . . Nouwen emphasized not only the importance of the incarnation of Christ as the one who showed human beings how to know and love God, but he also emphasized the kenosis of Christ, the emptying of himself for others through his life and death, as an example for Christians to imitate. Christ was at the center of most of Nouwen's thought about the Christian life, which he once defined as "living with Jesus at the center."[12]

"Nouwen was somewhat unusual in his attention to Scripture, especially as a Roman Catholic. He made reference to specific passages of Scripture over seven hundred times in the forty books that he wrote. Perhaps this is one reason why Nouwen was so appealing to evangelicals and widely read by them."[13] Henri uses the lessons and images found in Scripture to explain the relational nature of the persons of God, the Holy Trinity, and their relationship with us.

> Jesus is God-with-us, Emmanuel. The great mystery of God becoming human is God's desire to be loved by us. By becoming a vulner-

able child, completely dependent on human care, God wants to take away all distance between the human and the divine. . . . How can we be afraid of a God who wants to be "God-with-us" and wants us to become "Us-with-God"?
. . . God made a covenant with us. The word *covenant* means "coming together." God wants to come together with us. . . . In Jesus, God is born, grows to maturity, lives, suffers, and dies as we do. God is *God-with-us*. Finally, when Jesus leaves he promises the Holy Spirit. In the Holy Spirit, God reveals the full depth of the covenant. God wants to be as close to us as our breath. God wants to breathe in us, so that all we say, think, and do is completely inspired by God. God is *God-within-us*. Thus, God's covenant reveals to us how much God loves us.[14]

In his introduction to Henri's book *Jesus: A Gospel*, Michael O'Laughlin writes about how Henri touched his listeners when he spoke. "Henri had a way of making the Gospel come alive. He made us conscious of who we are and where we were at that moment. He made us aware of all that was going on in the world and what the Gospel had to say about our world and our lives."[15] However, Henri explains to his nephew Marc, sometime during the late 1980s, that it took time for his relationship with Jesus to grow and solidify.

Countless questions, problems, discussions, and difficulties always demand one's attention. Despite this, when I look back over the last thirty years of my life, I can say that, for me, the person of Jesus has come to be more and more important. Increasingly, what matters is getting to know Jesus and living in solidarity with him. At one time I was so immersed in problems of church and society that my whole life had become a sort of drawn-out, wearisome discussion. Jesus had been pushed into the background; he had himself become just another problem. Fortunately, it hasn't stayed that way. Jesus has stepped out in front again and asked me,

"And you, who do you say that I am?" It has become clearer to me than ever that my personal relationship with Jesus is the heart of my existence.[16]

"Jesus is not our Savior simply because of what he said to us or did for us. He is our Savior because what he said and did was said and done in obedience to his Father. . . . His obedience means a total, fearless listening to his loving Father. Between the Father and the Son there is only love."[17]

This love relationship inherent in the persons of the Trinity is something Henri believed was the model from which we are to live in our own relationships. In his diary *Sabbatical Journey*, Nouwen writes about a homily he gave during a small, intimate Mass with friends on the Feast of the Holy Trinity.

I tried to explain the mystery of the Trinity by saying that all human relationships are reflections of the relationships within God. God is the Lover, the Beloved, and the Love that binds us in unity. God invites us to be part of that inner movement of love so that we can truly become sons and daughters of the Father, sisters and brothers of the Son, and spouses of the Holy Spirit. Thus, all our human relationships can be lived *in* God, and as witness to God's divine presence in our lives.

I am deeply convinced that most human suffering comes from broken relationships. Anger, jealousy, resentment, and feelings of rejection all find their source in conflict between people who yearn for unity, community, and a deep sense of belonging. By claiming the Holy Trinity as home for our relational lives, we claim the truth that God gives us what we most desire and offers us the grace to forgive each other for not being perfect in love.[18]

"My hope is that the description of God's love in my life will give you the freedom and the courage to discover—and maybe also describe—God's love in yours."[19]

COMMUNITY

Besides the threads in his writing about who Jesus was and how God loved, Henri was very relational and believed that people of all ages long for intimacy, connectedness, and community. In order to understand the premise of community to which Henri refers, we listen to him reflecting on the story of the Visitation. Mary, the soon to be mother of Jesus, visits her cousin Elizabeth, who, like Mary, has become pregnant outside of the realm of human possibility.

> [T]wo women meet each other and affirm in each other the promise given to them. . . . Through these two women God has decided to change the course of history. Who could ever understand? Who could ever believe it? . . .
>
> Neither Mary nor Elizabeth had to wait in isolation. They could wait together and thus deepen in each other their faith in God, for whom nothing is impossible. Thus, God's most radical intervention into history was listened to and received in community.
>
> The story of the Visitation teaches me the meaning of friendship and community. How can I ever let God's grace fully work in my life unless I live in a community of people who can affirm it, deepen it, and strengthen it? We cannot live this new life alone. God does not want to isolate us by his grace. On the contrary, he wants us to form new friendships and a new community—holy places where his grace can grow to fullness and bear fruit.
>
> . . . God may choose us individually, but he always wants us to come together to allow his choice to come to maturity.[20]

Nouwen believed that when we support each other in our common journey, we create community. "Your own growth cannot take place without growth in others. You are part of a body. When you change, the whole body changes. It is very important for you to remain deeply connected with the larger community to which you belong."[21]

> Community is like a large mosaic. Each little piece seems so insignificant. One piece is bright red, another cold blue or dull green, another warm purple, another sharp yellow, another shining gold. Some look precious, others ordinary. Some look valuable, others worthless. Some look gaudy, others delicate. As individual stones, we can do little with them except compare them and judge their beauty and value. When, however, all these little stones are brought together in one big mosaic portraying the face of Christ, who would ever question the importance of any one of them? If one of them, even the least spectacular one, is missing, the face is incomplete. Together in the one mosaic, each little stone is indispensable and makes a unique contribution to the glory of God. That's community, a fellowship of little people who together make God visible in the world.[22]

In this way, the community does not exist for the sake of itself. As most of us have come to realize, it is often only in giving ourselves to others that we truly find ourselves. "A life well held is indeed a life for others. We stop wondering whether our life is better or worse than others and start seeing clearly that when we live our lives for others we not only claim our individuality but also proclaim our unique place in the mosaic of the human family."[23] However, in order to truly understand our identity, Nouwen continually challenges us to look back to the basic fact that we are all children of a God who loves us unconditionally. "At the core of my faith belongs the conviction that we are the beloved sons and daughters of God. One of the enormous spiritual tasks we have is to claim that and to live a life based on that knowledge and that's not very easy. In fact, most of us fail constantly to claim the truth of who we are."[24]

"In true community we are windows constantly offering each

other new views on the mystery of God's presence in our lives."[25]
Nouwen found in his own life that the mystery of God's presence
was revealed to him most profoundly through the people he came
to know and live with in the L'Arche community of Daybreak. In
an interview he gave in 1994, he reflects on not only the energy
or grace of God which sustains the community, but also on the
reality of what L'Arche attempts to proclaim to the world.

> Nouwen says he has come to realize that "Community can only be
> lived well if it comes out of communion with God, communion
> with Jesus, communion in the Spirit. You can only create a home
> for each other when you know your real home is in God."
>   L'Arche, he says, does not attempt to solve all the problems of
> the world. But it does want to be a beacon of hope to the world.
>   It is not just a safe home for its members, but "a community
> that radiates something into the world."[26]

"Where people have entered into the mind of Christ and no
longer think of their own interests first, the compassionate Christ
is made manifest and a healing presence is given to all."[27] This
healing presence can be experienced in the community in a number of ways, even though the struggles of the members remain.
The sharing of burdens, the acknowledgment of the presence of
the risen Lord, and the hope of healing in the light of the promise of eternal life—all often bring members of the community
both comfort and joy. Henri illustrates this while reflecting on an
intimate Easter morning Eucharist, celebrated around the table in
Madame Vanier's dining room in France.

> After the Gospel we spoke together about the resurrection. Liz,
> who works with many anguished people, said, "We have to keep
> rolling away the large stones that prevent people from coming out
> of their graves." Elizabeth, who lives with four handicapped peo-
> ple in a L'Arche foyer, said, "After the resurrection Jesus had break-

fast again with his friends and showed them the importance of the small, ordinary things of life." Sue, who is wondering if she might be called to go to Honduras and work with the L'Arche community there, said, "It is such a comfort to know that Jesus' wounds remain visible in his risen body. Our wounds are not taken away, but become sources of hope to others."

As everyone spoke, I felt very close to the Easter event. It was not a spectacular event forcing people to believe. Rather, it was an event for the friends of Jesus, for those who had known him, listened to him, and believed in him. It was a very intimate event: a word here, a gesture there, and a gradual awareness that something new was being born—small, hardly noticed, but with the potential to change the face of the earth. Mary of Magdala heard her name. John and Peter saw the empty grave. Jesus' friends felt their hearts burn in encounters that find expression in the remarkable words "He is risen." All had remained the same, while all had changed.

The five of us, sitting in a circle around the table with a little bread and a little wine, speaking softly about the way we were recognizing him in our lives, knew deep in our hearts that for us too all had changed, while all had remained the same. Our struggles are not ended. On Easter morning we can still feel the pains of the world, the pains of our family and friends, the pains of our hearts. They are still there and will be there for a long time. Still, all is different because we have met Jesus and he has spoken to us.

There was a simple, quiet joy among us and a deep sense of being loved by a love that is stronger, much stronger, than death.[28]

Henri continues to give us food for thought about what community really is.

[C]ommunity, like solitude, is primarily a quality of the heart. . . . [C]ommunity does not necessarily mean being physically together. We can well live in community while being physically alone. In such a situation, we can act freely, speak honestly, and suffer patiently, because of the intimate bond of love that unites us with others even when time and place separate us from them. The community of love stretches out not only beyond the boundaries of countries and continents, but also beyond the boundaries of decades and centuries. Not only the awareness of those who are far away but also the memory of those who lived long ago can lead us into a healing, sustaining, and guiding community. The space for God in community transcends all limits of time and place.[29]

PRAYER AND SOLITUDE

We live in a world filled with busyness, competition, cynicism, and rejection. Henri promoted setting aside time in our lives for solitude, silence and prayer, in order to hear the voice of the one who calls us "Beloved."

Through the discipline of solitude we discover space for God in our innermost being. Through the discipline of community we discover a place for God in our life together. Both disciplines belong together precisely because the space within us and the space among us are the same space.

It is in this divine space that God's Spirit prays in us. Prayer is first and foremost the active presence of the Holy Spirit in our personal and communal lives.[30]

In solitude we can listen to the voice of him who spoke to us before we could speak a word, who healed us before we could make any gesture to help, who set us free long before we could free others, and who loved us long before we could give love to anyone. It is in this solitude that we discover that being is more important than having, and that we are worth more than the result of our efforts. In solitude we discover that our life is not a possession to be defended, but a gift to be shared. It's there that we recognize that the healing words we speak are not just our own, but are given to us; that the love we can express is part of a greater love; and that the new life we bring forth is not a property to cling to, but a gift to be received.

In solitude we become aware that our worth is not the same as our usefulness.[31]

Nouwen explains to us that it is the Spirit of God who initiates prayer, and that we have to become quiet and open ourselves to the Spirit, allowing space in our hearts for God to speak to us and to act out of. "[T]o see or hear God is not a human possibility. It is a divine sensitivity. It is the Spirit of God who gives us eyes to see and ears to hear, who allows us to see and hear God in every person we serve. . . . But when we have not met God in the center of our own hearts, we cannot expect to meet God in the busyness of our daily lives."[32] The people we meet and minister to in our lives need both our presence and our prayer. We are to take them and their needs back to God, where God meets us in the solitude of our hearts.

The goal of our life is not people. It is God. Only in God shall we find the rest we seek. It is therefore to solitude that we must return, not alone, but with all those whom we embrace through our min- istry. This return continues until the time when the same Lord who sent us into the world calls us back to be with him in a never-end- ing communion.[33]

Yet Nouwen, in the spirit of the Desert Fathers, also refers to solitude as the true "furnace of transformation." He tells us that if we do not enter the furnace which changes and transforms us, we will remain victims of what our society dictates to us and be caught up in the illusions of the false self. "Solitude is the place of the great struggle and the great encounter—the struggle against the compulsions of the false self, and the encounter with the lov- ing God who offers himself as the substance of the new self."[34]

Through perseverance in seeking solitude, silence, and prayer, we will hear the voice of the Spirit, who will not only reveal our true identity to us as God's beloved children but also change our hearts so that we can live in solidarity with all others who share the same struggles and weaknesses as ourselves. "Compassion is the fruit of solitude and the basis of all ministry. The purification and transformation that take place in solitude manifest themselves in compassion."[35]

COMPASSION

"Be compassionate just as your Father is compassionate." (Luke 6:36) That is the core message of the Gospel. The way human beings are called to love one another is God's way. We are called to love one another with the same selfless outgoing love that we see in Rembrandt's depiction of the father. The compassion with which we are to love cannot be based upon a competitive lifestyle. It has to be this absolute compassion in which no trace of competition can be found. It has to be this radical love of enemy. If we are not only to be received by God, but also to receive as God, we must become like God and see the world through God's eyes.[36]

Compassion is a value which is misunderstood. To be compassionate is something other than feeling sorry for someone or having pity on them. Pity would suggest distance, and in some sense condescendence. "I often act with pity. I give some money to a beggar on the streets of Toronto, or New York City, but I do not look him in his eyes, sit down with him, or talk with him. I am too busy to really pay attention to the man who reaches out to me. My money replaces my personal attention and gives me an excuse to walk on."[37]

However, compassion means to become vulnerable ourselves and to come close to the one who suffers. We can be that way with one another only when the other ceases to be "someone else" and becomes like us. We find it is easier to show pity than compassion, because the suffering person calls us to be aware of our own suffering. There is much grief and pain in all of our lives, and yet it is a blessing when we do not have to live it alone. Caring for another with the eyes and heart of God transforms pity into compassion. "By viewing compassion as an obedient response to our loving God, we avoid the constant temptation to see it as a noble act of self-sacrifice."[38]

> In Jesus, God's compassion is revealed as suffering with us in obedience. Jesus is not a courageous hero whose act of emptying and humbling himself earns adoration and praise. He is not a super social worker, a super doctor, or a super helper. He is not a great hero who performs acts of self-denial that no one can imitate. Jesus is neither a spiritual giant nor a superstar whose compassion makes us jealous and creates in us the competitive desire to get as far, high, or deep as he did. No, Jesus is the obedient servant who hears the call and desires to respond even when it leads him to pain and suffering. This desire is not to experience pain, but to give his full undivided attention to the voice of his beloved Father.[39]

If we look to Jesus as our model, we too will be called to service and servanthood. "Radical servanthood does not make sense unless we introduce a new level of understanding and see it as the way to encounter God. . . . Here we are touching the profound spiritual truth that service is an expression of the search for God and not just of the desire to bring about individual or social change."[40] Every time we act out of this understanding of compassion, we reveal the gentle presence of our compassionate God in the midst of our broken world.

Being called to live compassionate lives, to truly manifest the compassion of a loving God in all situations and to everyone, is no doubt a great challenge. It is something we can aspire to with hope. Nouwen points us in the right direction by reminding us of the basics: (1) allowing ourselves to accept and internalize our true identity as God's "Beloved"; (2) taking the time through prayer and solitude to hear the voice of love within us; (3) engaging ourselves in relationships and community which support and feed our call to radical servanthood; and (4) not being afraid to be vulnerable with those who are suffering in order to journey with them in compassion.

Much of what this encompasses is shared in the following story, written by Jan Davis, a wife, mother, and spiritual director in San Antonio.

> I walked into the hospital room to visit my cousin Jean Marie. She told me to come closer so she could smell my perfume. Spunky girl, that was her trick to get me to come near. "What's the good word for today?" she asked, apparently spotting my prayer book in my purse. She almost made me uncomfortable; she could see more about me than I wanted her to. "You brought the Good Word," she repeated and asked me to read to her the last psalm, Psalm 150. It was her favorite, she said. Her terminal heart disease did not dim the vision of the final triumph, "Let everything that has breath praise the Lord. Alleluia!" that soon would be hers in a final and complete way. Even though young, forty-six, and a good candidate for a heart transplant, she said she didn't want someone else's heart.
>
> Only now does it become clear to me how Jean Marie could see with the eyes of her heart. For some it would be a blessing; for others, a burden; for others, a vocation. Henri Nouwen said, "My deepest vocation is to be a witness to the glimpses of God I have been allowed to catch."[41]

Henri's spirituality has been captured through his diligence in writing down his experiences and insights, in order to witness to them and share them with the world. His work continues to reach out and inspire many people, particularly those who face the issues and questions surrounding how to befriend death, how to die well, and how to care well.

Chapter Three

BEFRIENDING DEATH

It seems indeed important that we face death before we are in any real danger of dying and reflect on our mortality before all our conscious and unconscious energy is directed to the struggle to survive. It is important to be prepared for death, very important; but if we start thinking about it only when we are terminally ill, our reflections will not give us the support we need.

Henri Nouwen, *A Letter of Consolation*

Six months after the death of his mother in 1978, Henri wrote to his father in an effort to console him. He did not initially intend that the letter would be published, but eventually did so with the desire to offer it to all those who suffer the pain that death can bring, and who search for new life. As he tries to journey through his grief and make sense of his beloved mother's death, he explains to his father that it seems to be an opportune time for both of them to confront their own deaths.

I think, then, that our first task is to befriend death. I like that expression "to befriend." I first heard it used by Jungian analyst James Hillman when he attended a seminar I taught on Christian Spirituality at Yale Divinity School. He emphasized the importance of "befriending": befriending your dreams, befriending your shadow, befriending your unconscious. He made it convincingly clear that in order to become full human beings, we have to claim the totality of our experience; we come to maturity by integrating not only the light but also the dark side of our story into our selfhood. . . . And isn't death, the frightening unknown that lurks in the depths of our unconscious minds, like a great shadow that we perceive only dimly in our dreams? Befriending death seems to be the basis of all other forms of befriending.[1]

He tried to explain to his father the power one can have over death itself by befriending one's own death, using the example of a Dutchman named Floris Bakels, whose concentration camp diary was published under the title *Nacht und Nebel* (Night and Fog).

He makes very clear what power a man can have who has befriended his own death. . . . Wouldn't you say that Floris Bakels was able to survive the horrors of Dachau and other camps and write about it thirty-two years later precisely because he had befriended death? It seems, at least to me, that Floris Bakels said in many different ways to his SS captors, "You have no power over me, because I have already died."[2]

Nouwen believed that if we could relate to death as a familiar guest instead of a threatening stranger, we would be able to shed many of our doubts and insecurities, face our mortality, and live as free people.

True freedom is the freedom of the children of God. To reach that freedom requires a lifelong discipline since so much in our world militates against it. The political, economic, social, and even religious powers surrounding us all want to keep us in bondage so that we will obey their commands and be dependent on their rewards.

But the spiritual truth that leads to freedom is the truth that we belong not to the world but to God, whose beloved children we are. By living lives in which we keep returning to that truth in word and deed, we will gradually grow into our true freedom.[3]

Nouwen also believed that a large part of befriending death had to do with love. Henri loved his mother deeply, and shared with his father the notion that their married love, which had grown over forty-seven years, was so strong that it would never end, surviving even death itself. Now with his mother's passing, the real absurdity of death was revealed, causing them both to ask the question, "Why could our love not prevent her from dying?"

"Real love says, 'Forever.' Love will always reach out toward the eternal. Love comes from that place within us where death cannot enter. Love does not accept the limits of hours, days, weeks, months, years, or centuries. Love is not willing to be imprisoned by time."[4] Indeed, we hear this in the Song of Solomon, "For love is strong as death" (Song of Sol. 8:6 NRSV).

Yet, the same love that reveals the absurdity of death also allows us to befriend death. The same love that forms the basis of our grief is also the basis of our hope; the same love that makes us cry out in pain also must enable us to develop a liberating intimacy with our own most basic brokenness. But our faith in him whose love overcame death and who rose from the grave on the third day converts this contradiction into a paradox, the most healing paradox of our existence.

Floris Bakels experienced this in a unique way. He came to see and feel that the power of love is stronger than the power of death and that it is indeed true that "God is love." Surrounded by people dying from hunger, torture, and total exhaustion, and knowing quite well that any hour could be his hour to die, he found in the core of his being a love so strong and so profound that the fear of death lost its power over him. . . . [I]t was the very concrete, real, and intimate love of Jesus Christ, Son of God and redeemer of the world. With his whole being he knew that he was loved with an infinite love, held in an eternal embrace and surrounded by an unconditional care. . . . The more deeply and fully he experienced Christ's love, the more he came to see that the many loves in his life—the love of his parents, his brother and sisters, his wife, and his friends—were reflections of the great "first" love of God.

I am convinced that it was the deeply felt love of God—felt in and through Jesus Christ—that allowed Floris Bakels to face his own death and the deaths of others so directly. It was this love that gave him the freedom and energy to help people in agony and made it possible for him to resume a normal life after he returned from the hell of Dachau.[5]

This story beautifully illustrates how befriending our death is the key which unlocks the door to being able to live our earthly life in freedom. Yet, the question which begs to be asked is, "How does someone begin to befriend their death?"

CLAIMING OUR BELOVEDNESS

Perhaps we cannot befriend death until we fully befriend life— being able to identify who we really are and why we're here. Of course these are the "big" questions of life, which Henri himself pondered and addressed through his writings over many years. "During our short lives the question that guides much of our behavior is: 'Who are we?' Although we may seldom pose that question in a formal way, we live it very concretely in our day-to-day decisions."[6]

The spiritual life requires a constant claiming of our true identity. Our true identity is that we are God's children, the beloved sons and daughters of our heavenly Father. Jesus' life reveals to us this mysterious truth. After Jesus was baptized in the Jordan by John, as he was coming up out of the water, he saw the heavens torn apart and the Spirit, like a dove, descending on him. And a voice came from heaven: "You are my Son, the Beloved; my favor rests on you." (Mark 1:10–11). This is the decisive moment of Jesus' life. His true identity is declared to him. He is the Beloved of God. As "the Beloved" he is being sent into the world so that through him all people will discover and claim their own belovedness.[7]

Perhaps we haven't thought about this notion before, that God loves us and desires to be loved by us, even infinitely more than we think we love God. To be someone's "beloved" denotes a certain strength, a depth, and an everlasting, unconditional commitment. Can we listen, as Jesus did, and hear God call us "Beloved"? Can we begin to identify ourselves first and foremost as being beloved children of God? Henri intently desired that all persons should come to an understanding of seeing themselves in this way; he revisited this concept in many of his books.

However, Henri also noted that the voice calling us "Beloved" is hard for us to hear in our everyday world. Loud are the voices which tell us we are "worthless," "not rich enough," "not powerful enough," "not lovable enough," "not attractive enough." Deep are the wounds we all carry from the times we felt we didn't measure up to the expectations of our parents, our teachers, our employers, or our friends. We spend our lives trying to prove to ourselves, and to others, that we are somebody, that we are worthy, that we are lovable. We keep forgetting who we really are and waste much time and energy proving what we do not need to prove. We are God's chosen ones, the beloved sons and daughters of God—not because we have proven ourselves worthy of God's love, but because God chose us first.

We can look to the example of Jesus to help us understand this further. In Luke's Gospel, after Jesus' baptism in the Jordan and hearing God's voice call him "my Beloved," Satan tempted Jesus to prove who he was. "Prove that you are the beloved by changing these stones into bread." But, Jesus knew that he didn't have to prove anything to Satan or to anyone else. He believed he was the beloved because he had heard it spoken by the One

who sent him. Henri, in explaining this notion to an audience at
the U.S. National Catholic AIDS Network in July of 1995, stated,
"Listen to him. I want you to know that we are not just speaking
about Jesus. We are speaking about us. Because Jesus came to
share his identity with us, to give us his Christhood, to give us this
anointing, to make us the beloved sons and daughters of God and
to help us claim the truth."[8]

Henri went on to tell them:

> [Y]our belovedness precedes your births. You are the beloved before
> you are born. You are the beloved before your father and mother,
> brother, sister, or church loves you or wants you or hurts you. You
> are the beloved because you belong to God for all eternity.
>
> You were the beloved before you were born, and you will be
> the beloved after you die. That's the truth of your identity. That's
> who you are whether you feel bad or not bad, or whatever the
> world makes you feel or think or experience. You belong to God
> from eternity to eternity. Life is just an interruption of eternity, just
> a little opportunity for a few years to say, "I love you, too."[9]

"The unfathomable mystery of God is that God is a Lover
who wants to be loved. The one who created us is waiting for our
response to the love that gave us our being. God not only says:
'You are my Beloved.' God also asks: 'Do you love me?' and offers
us countless chances to say 'Yes.' That is the spiritual life: the
chance to say 'Yes' to our inner truth."[10]

If we understand our life and identity in this way, then everything we do can be an expression of our "yes" to God. Our growing up and leaving home, finding a career, being praised and
being rejected, walking and playing, resting and praying, becoming ill and being healed, and even living and dying, all become
expressions of that Divine question: "Do you love me?" At every
turn in the journey we have the choice and the freedom to say
"yes" or "no."

The change of which I speak is the change from living a life as a painful test to prove that you deserve to be loved, to living it as an unceasing "Yes" to the truth of that Belovedness. Put simply, life is a God-given opportunity to become who we are, to affirm our own true spiritual nature, claim our truth, appropriate and integrate the reality of our being, but, most of all, to say "Yes" to the One who calls us the Beloved.[11]

If living is truly as simple as this, why do we find it so difficult to achieve? Throughout his life, Henri, like all of us, struggled with the weaknesses inherent in his humanity and found it difficult to continually say "yes" to God. He often found himself feeling distraught, depressed, and alone, despite the "head knowledge" that he was indeed loved unconditionally by God. With his mind, he understood that Jesus could give him a "peace that the world cannot give," but he still looked to outside projects and other people to satisfy his heart's longing for peace and love.

Our spiritual journey is a life-long adventure in continuously moving this knowledge from our head down into our heart. As we do so, we will not only come to know and feel and trust the love of God with every fiber of our being, but we will also aspire to live out of that center. "In every phase of my search I've discovered also that Jesus Christ stands at the center of my seeking. If you were to ask me point-blank, 'What does it mean to you to live spiritually?' I would have to reply, 'Living with Jesus at the center.' "[12]

Living spiritually is more than living physically, intellectually, or emotionally. It embraces all that, but it is larger, deeper, and wider. It concerns the core of your humanity. It is possible to lead a very wholesome, emotionally rich, and "sensible" life without being a spiritual person: that is, without knowledge or personal experience of the terrain where the meaning and goal of our human existence are hidden.

The spiritual life has to do with the heart of existence. This is a good word. By heart I do not mean the seat of our feelings as opposed to the seat of our thoughts; I mean the center of our being, that place where we are most ourselves, where we are most human, where we are most real. In that sense the heart is the focus of the spiritual life.[13]

To speak of the heart in this way, is to understand it to be the dwelling place of God, the place where God resides or "abides." Jesus tells us, "As the Father has loved me, so I have loved you; abide in my love. If you keep my commandments, you will abide in my love, just as I have kept my Father's commandments and abide in his love" (Jn 15:9–10 NRSV).

Knowing this truth, and being able to honor it in our living, remains a challenge. During what was to be the final year of his life, Henri had been on sabbatical from being the pastor of Daybreak. He kept a diary every day of his thoughts, feelings, and numerous encounters with friends and family that called him to travel extensively. Throughout this time he also wrote four new books. After I read *Sabbatical Journey*, the account of that extremely busy year, it was easy to see why he often experienced fatigue. Failing to heed his body's warnings to slow down, he died suddenly of a heart attack three weeks after returning to Daybreak. In this diary, there are countless entries indicating that although he knew himself to be God's beloved, he failed to be able to live it fully. One of these is found in the entry from Tuesday, May 14.

Jesus invites me to abide in his love. That means to dwell with all that I am in him. It is an invitation to a total belonging, to full intimacy, to an unlimited being-with.

The anxiety that has plagued me during the last week shows that a great part of me is not yet "abiding" in Jesus. My mind and heart keep running away from my true dwelling place, and they explore strange lands where I end up in anger, resentment, lust, fear, and anguish. I know that living a spiritual life means bringing every part of myself home to where it belongs.

. . . Somehow I keep living as if there are other sources of life that I must explore, outside of Jesus. But Jesus keeps saying, "Come back to me, give me all your burdens, all your worries, fears, and anxieties. Trust that with me you will find rest." I am struggling to listen to that voice of love and to trust in its healing power.

I deeply know that I have a home in Jesus, just as Jesus has a home in God. I know, too, that when I abide in Jesus I abide with him in God. . . . My true spiritual work is to let myself be loved, fully and completely, and to trust that in love I will come to the fulfillment of my vocation. I keep trying to bring my wandering, restless, anxious self home, so that I can rest there in the embrace of love.[14]

Isn't that really the vocation of all of us? To keep trying, in our anxiety and busyness, to bring ourselves home and rest there often in the embrace of God's love? How do we do that? How does someone keep their focus set on the love and call of God? How do we come to know and love this God in return, to recognize God's voice and trust God's promises?

KNOWING OUR BELOVEDNESS THROUGH PRAYER

Henri believed wholeheartedly that one of the most important ways to develop an intimate relationship with this God of love was through solitude and prayer. "Nobody has to prove to me that prayer makes a difference. Without prayer I become irritable, tired, heavy of heart, and I lose the Spirit who directs my attention to the needs of others instead of my own. Without prayer, my attention moves to my own preoccupation."[15]

We, therefore, need discipline to keep living truthfully and not succumb to the endless seductions of our society. Wherever we are there are voices saying: "Go here, go there, buy this, buy that, get to know him, get to know her, don't miss this, don't miss that," and so on and on. These voices keep pulling us away from that soft gentle voice that speaks in the center of our being: "You are my beloved, on you my favor rests."

Prayer is the discipline of listening to that voice of love. Jesus spent many nights in prayer listening to the voice that had spoken to him at the Jordan River. We too must pray. Without prayer we become deaf to the voice of love and become confused by the many competing voices asking for our attention. How difficult this is! When we sit down for half an hour—without talking to someone, listening to music, watching television, or reading a book—and try to become very still, we often find ourselves so overwhelmed by our noisy inner voices that we can hardly wait to get busy and distracted again. . . . But God is greater than our hearts and minds and keeps calling us the beloved . . . far beyond all feelings and thoughts.[16]

Many of us might feel that prayer is a daunting task. Perhaps we are afraid to pray, to face God with our fears and doubts. Perhaps we don't think we know how to pray. Maybe we have felt that all our life our prayers have fallen on deaf ears. Henri wrote many books which dealt specifically with prayer, solitude, and the need for this in our lives. He, along with many others through the centuries, has given us a wealth of insight that helps us find our own comfortable way to converse with God. As pilgrims, we will spend our entire lives seeking ways to experience the connection and communion that awaits us if we only stop long enough to spend time with God in our hearts, the place God calls "home."

Many approach prayer as being a litany of petitions, a grocery list of wants and needs for God to fill for us. Or, because we essentially fear God and feel we are not worthy of God's unconditional love, we often come to God cowering in shame and guilt, afraid to let God forgive us or love us and even deny God the chance to give us the grace and strength we need to grow. Throughout many of Henri's books he spoke of his own personal struggles with prayer. Perhaps a few of his reflections may be able to help us in our own attempts to claim our belovedness and be present to this God who loves us abundantly and whose only desire is to be in communion with us and be loved in return.

Henri reminds us that although we are busy, if we do not pray, "we are constantly tempted to let ourselves be disconnected from the source of our lives."[17]

In a diary entry Henri writes:

Prayer continues to be very difficult. Still, every morning when I walk in the garden of La Ferme saying the rosary and spending an hour in the oratory in God's presence, I know that I am not wasting my time. Though I am terribly distracted, I know that God's spirit is at work in me. Though I have no deeply religious insights or feelings, I am aware of the peace beyond thoughts and emotions. Though my early-morning prayer seems quite unsuccessful, I always look forward to it and guard it as a special time. . . . We must pray not first of all because it feels good or helps, but because God loves us and wants our attention.[18]

While living at the Abbey of the Genesee in 1979, he wrote:

Dear Lord, this afternoon I shared my feelings of guilt and sinfulness with one of the monks. He gave me good advice. He kept urging me to move away continually from introspection and self-preoccupation and to concentrate on expressing my love for you.[19]

In this same vein, Henri describes the advice he once received from Mother Teresa of Calcutta:

When I explained to her all my problems and struggles with elaborate details and asked for her insights, she simply said: "If you spend one hour a day in contemplative prayer and never do anything which you know is wrong, you will be all right." With these words she answered none as well as all of my problems at the same time. It was now up to me to be willing to move to the place where that answer could be heard.[20]

She answers them [questions brought to her] with a logic, from a perspective, and in a place that remains unfamiliar to most of us. It is a divine logic, a divine perspective, a divine place. . . . Like Jesus himself, she challenges her listeners to move with her to that place where things can be seen as God sees them.[21]

At first, her answer didn't seem to fit my question, but then I began to see that her answer came from God's place and not from the place of my complaints. Most of the time we respond to questions from below with answers from below. The result is more questions and more answers and, often, more confusion.

Mother Teresa's answer was like a flash of lightning in my darkness. I suddenly knew the truth about myself.[22]

Once we are able to begin to look at things through God's eyes, as Mother Teresa expresses, we then begin to see that all of our brothers and sisters are also as beloved as we are!

UNDERSTANDING OUR LIFE AS MISSION

Having explored with Henri the question of who we are, we see ourselves now as the beloved children of God. We understand our God to be One who created us out of love, who lives in our hearts, and continues to love us unconditionally throughout our earthly life and into eternity. Henri gives us the courage and the insights now to be able to ask, *"Why are we here?"*

If you believe that you are beloved before you are born, you can suddenly realize that life is a mission. You are sent here just for a little bit, for 20, 30, 40, 50 years. It doesn't matter. You are sent into this world to make your brothers and sisters know that they are as beloved as you are, that they are beloved sons and daughters and belong together. You're sent into this world to be people of reconcil-iation. You are sent to heal, to break down the walls between all the categories that you can think about—young, old, black, white, gay, straight—whatever divisions you can come up with—Serb, Croat, Muslim, Catholic, Protestant, Hindu, Buddhist. Before all those dis-tinctions and walls and separations there is unity. Out of that experi-ence of unity that is there before you are born, you can go into this world for a little while and can claim that every human being belongs to that same heart that beats from eternity to eternity.

. . . If you are chosen in the heart of God, you have eyes to see the chosenness of others.[23]

"To befriend death, we must claim that we are children of God, sisters and brothers of all people, and parents of generations yet to come. In so doing, we liberate our death from its absurdity and make it the gateway to a new life."[24]

Henri expresses the need to also experience deep joy in realiz-ing we are unique individuals—children of a God who loves us for who we are. We are joyful as we mark the milestones which devel-op our own identity; we celebrate our accomplishments and achievements, ultimately helping us dispel self-doubts and build self-confidence. "This is the joy of having 'made it,' the joy of being recognized for making a difference. We all wait for this joy some-where, somehow. It remains the joy of the one who said, 'I thank you God, that I am not like everyone else' (Luke 18:11–12)."[25]

The other kind of joy is harder to describe but easier to find. It is the joy of being the brother or sister of all people . . . and only a few people ever truly find it. This is the joy of being a part of that vast variety of people—of all ages, colors, and religions—who together form the human family. This is the immense joy of being a member of the human race.

At several times in my life, I have tasted this joy. I felt it most acutely in 1964, when I walked with thousands of people in Alabama from Selma to Montgomery in a civil rights march led by

Martin Luther King, Jr. I will never forget the joy I experienced during that march. I had come by myself. Nobody knew me—nobody
had ever heard of me—but when we walked together and put our
arms around each other's shoulders and sang "We shall overcome
one day," I experienced a joy I had never experienced before in my
life. I said to myself, "Yes, yes, I belong; these are my people. They
may have a differently-colored skin, a different religion, a different
way of life, but they are my brothers and sisters. They love me, and
I love them. Their smiles and tears are my smiles and tears; their
prayers and prophecies are my prayers and prophecies; their
anguish and hope are my anguish and hope. I am one with them."
     In an instant, all differences seemed to melt away as snow in
the sun . . . and I felt surrounded by the welcoming arms of all
humanity.[26]

Henri was convinced that it is this deeply felt, immense sense
of joy—of belonging to one human family, and being the same as
others—that allows us to die well.

The great gift hidden in our dying is the gift of unity with all people. However different we are, we were all born powerless, and we
all die powerless, and the little differences we live in between dwin-
dle in the light of this enormous truth. . . . Our great challenge is
to discover this truth as a source of immense joy that will set us free
to embrace our mortality with the awareness that we will make our
passage to new life in solidarity with all the people of the earth.[27]

When Henri started to reflect on his own dying in preparation for writing *Our Greatest Gift,* the sense of powerlessness it
would bring was profound for him.

Gradually, my body will lose its strength, my mind its flexibility; I will
lose family and friends; I will become less relevant to society and be
forgotten by most; I will have to depend increasingly on the help of

others; and, in the end, I will have to let go of everything and be carried into the completely unknown. Am I willing to make that journey? Am I willing to let go of whatever power I have left, to unclench my fists and trust in the grace hidden in complete powerlessness?[28]

What helped him to discover the strength to do so, was the realization that everyone in the human family shares the same fate.

We all die poor. When we come to our final hours, nothing can help us survive. No amount of money, power, or influence can keep us from dying. This is true poverty. But Jesus said, "Blessed are you who are poor; the kingdom of God is yours" (Luke 6:20). There is a blessing hidden in the poverty of dying. It is the blessing that makes us brothers and sisters in the same Kingdom. It is the blessing we receive from others who die. It is the blessing we give to others when our time to die has come. It is the blessing that comes from the God whose life is everlasting. It is the blessing that reaches far beyond our birth and death. It is the blessing that carries us safely from eternity to eternity.[29]

Some of us die earlier, others later; some after a short life, others after a long life; some after an illness, others suddenly and unexpectedly. But all of us will die and participate in the same end. . . . This communion with the whole human family, this profound sense of belonging to each other, takes the sting out of dying and points us far beyond the limits of our chronology. Somehow, we know that our bond with one another is stronger than death.

We touch here the core of Jesus' message. Jesus didn't come to simply point us away from this world by promising a new life after death. He came to make us aware that, as children of his God, we are all his brothers and sisters, all brothers and sisters of each other; we can, therefore, live our lives together without fear of death. He wants us not only to participate in his divine childhood, but also to enjoy fully the brotherhood and sisterhood that emerges from this shared childhood. He says to us, "Just as the Father has loved me, so I have loved you" (John 15:9), and "You must love one another, just as I have loved you" (John 13:34).[30]

BELIEVING THAT OUR LIVES BEAR FRUIT

Henri came to understand, however, that not only are we called to be brothers and sisters, loving and supporting one another in our living and our dying, but we are also the parents of generations to come. No matter at what age we die, or whether we actually parent any children, our living and our dying form a legacy for those who come after us. This legacy, or fruitfulness, is seldom realized until long after we have gone. Nouwen experienced this in a very real way as he shared in the journey of his sister-in-law Marina, who suffered from cancer. Marina was a teacher, who often expressed herself through painting and poetry. As she prepared to die at the age of forty-eight, her poems in particular became the direct fruit of her struggle to befriend death.

As I have seen Marina prepare herself for her death, I have gradually realized that she is making her own dying a gift for others—not only for my brother Paul, not only for her family and friends, but also for the nurses and doctors and the many circles of people with whom she has spoken and shared her poems. Having taught all her life, she now teaches through her preparation for death. It strikes me that her successes and accomplishments will probably soon be forgotten, but the fruits of her dying may well last a long time. . . . She has shown me, in a whole new way, what it means to die for others. It means to become the parent of future generations.[31]

Again, Henri refers to Sacred Scripture and the life and death of Jesus Christ to help us to understand how we can make the journey through the end of our earthly lives fruitful for those we

leave behind and for those who come after us. In trying to explain
his imminent death to his friends and disciples, Jesus acknowl-
edged their sorrow and sadness but assured them it would bring
something good.

> Still, I am telling you the truth: it is for your own good that I am
> going, because unless I go, the Spirit will not come to you; but if I
> go, I will send him to you. . . . I shall have many things to say to
> you but they would be too much for you to bear now. However,
> when the Spirit of truth comes he will lead you to the complete
> truth, since he will not be speaking of his own accord, but will say
> only what he has been told; and he will reveal to you the things to
> come. (John 16:7, 13)[32]

Henri makes the connection that by sharing her poems and
paintings, Marina will also give new life to those who mourn her
death. "Isn't 'sending the Spirit' the best expression for not leaving
those you love alone but offering them a new bond, deeper than
the bond that existed in life? Doesn't 'dying for others' mean
dying so that others can continue to live, strengthened by the
Spirit of our love?"[33]

One of the ways the Spirit of our love manifests itself is
through memory. In his book *The Living Reminder* Nouwen speaks
about its importance.

> One of the mysteries of life is that memory can often bring us
> closer to each other than can physical presence. Physical presence
> not only invites but also blocks intimate communication. In our
> preresurrection state our bodies hide as much as they reveal.
> Indeed, many of our disappointments and frustrations in life are
> related to the fact that seeing and touching each other does not
> always create the closeness we seek. The more experience in liv-
> ing we have, the more we sense that closeness grows in the con-
> tinuous interplay between presence and absence.

In absence, from a distance, in memory, we see each other in a new way. We are less distracted by each other's idiosyncrasies and are better able to see and understand each other's inner core.

When I am away from home, I often express myself in letters in a much more intimate way than when I am with my family . . .

In memory we are able to be in touch with each other's spirit, with that reality in each other which enables an always deepening communication. There is little doubt that memory can distort, falsify, and cause selective perception. But that is only one aspect of memory. Memory also clarifies, purifies, brings into focus, and calls to the foreground hidden gifts. When a mother and father think of their children who have left home, when a child remembers his parents, when a husband and wife call each other to mind during long periods of absence, when friends recall their friends, it is often the very best that is evoked and the real beauty of the other that breaks through into consciousness. When we remember each other with love we evoke each other's spirit and so enter into a new intimacy, a spiritual union with each other.[34]

There are countless other ways the fruitfulness of our life is experienced both during our lifetime and after we die. In his book *Lifesigns,* Nouwen talks about intimacy, fecundity, and ecstasy. "Fecundity" is a rather archaic term which we tend not to use now, but Nouwen explains the need to rediscover it, as it pertains to being "fruitful." He uses the verse, "Those who abide in me and I in them bear much fruit" (Jn 15:5 NRSV), to speak of the fruit which puts us in touch with our deepest human potential to bring forth life.

Much pain in the world of today is directly caused by this deep sense of worthlessness. Countless people experience their existence as dull, boring, stagnant, and routine. They lack inner vitality, a deep desire to be alive. For them, every day is just another day, often filled with many things to do but seldom offering profound human satisfaction.

This is the experience of living without bearing fruit. But, fortunately, some men and women have a deep sense of their value—precisely because they are in touch with the life-giving quality of their existence. Their joy brings forth joy, and their peace brings forth peace.
They make us aware of the holy contagiousness of all that lives.[35]

The beauty of life is that long after we die, we continue to
bear fruit. The legacy we leave for the people we have known
finds its fullness after we are gone. Many times we also affect the
lives of people we have never even met. The way they live,
inspired by the way we lived, carries on into eternity. Jesus said,
"Very truly, I tell you, unless a grain of wheat falls into the earth
and dies, it remains just a single grain; but if it dies, it bears much
fruit" (Jn 12:24 NRSV). Henri knew that long after his mother
died he continued to make decisions guided by her spirit, the
Spirit of Jesus which she continued to send to him. Many of us
know that to be true in our own lives as the presence and wisdom
of the loved ones who formed us continues to live in our hearts
and actions. We remember them, not because they left us, but
because they changed us.

Henri speaks so beautifully of this fruitfulness with his reflection on the life and death of Maurice Gould.

Maurice had made his home in the L'Arche Daybreak community in
Toronto for fourteen years. He was known for his joyfulness, gentleness, and love of home. The countless people who met him over
the years speak about him with much endearment. Somehow his
condition—Down's syndrome—seemed only the other side of his
great gift: to give and receive love. . . .

The days that followed were full of sorrow and joy. Moe was
dead, but it seemed as if new life became immediately visible.
Telephone calls were made to friends far and wide; letters were
written. Most of all, people came together to pray, to eat, to tell
stories, to look at pictures—to remember with smiles and tears.

Of all the days that I have lived at Daybreak, those after Moe's death belong to the most intimate, the most uniting, and, in a strange way, the most sacred. A man who, through his fragility and weakness, had helped us create community during his life did so even more through his death. . . . [W]e shared a deep sense that not only does life lead to death, but death leads to new life. The spirit of gentleness and kindness that surrounded and pervaded our conversation, the spirit of forgiveness and healing that touched each of us, and most of all the spirit of unity and communion that bound us together in a new way—that spirit was gratefully received as a gift of Moe who was dead and yet very much alive.[36]

The time we spend here on earth is only a blink of an eye in the realm of eternity.

Our short lives on earth are sowing times. If there were no resurrection of the dead, everything we live on earth would come to nothing. How can we believe in a God who loves us unconditionally if all the joys and pains of our lives are in vain[?] . . . This wonderful knowledge that nothing we live in our bodies is lived in vain holds a call for us to live every moment as a seed of eternity.[37]

Henri goes on to explain how God's time is "timeless."

There is no "after" after death. Words like after and before belong to our mortal life, our life in time and space. Death frees us from the boundaries of chronology and brings us into God's "time," which is timeless. Speculations about the afterlife, therefore, are little more than that: speculations. Beyond death there is no "first" and "later," no "here" and "there," no "past," "present," or "future." God is all in all. The end of time, the resurrection of the body, and the glorious coming again of Jesus are no longer separated by time for those who are no longer in time.

For us who still live in time, it is important not to act as if the new life in Christ is something we can comprehend or explain. God's heart and mind are greater than ours. All that is asked of us is trust.[38]

We can look again at the life of Jesus to help us understand this concept. He did not live a long life, he never traveled outside of his own country, and the people who met him during his lifetime seemed to hardly understand him. When he died, only a handful of his followers remained faithful to him. By our standards, his life was a failure. He had no success, no popularity, and no power when he was beaten and crucified. Still, few lives have been so fruitful, and affected the thinking and feeling of others so tremendously. No other life has so profoundly shaped future cultures and influenced the patterns of human relationships. Over and over, Jesus himself stressed to his followers that the fruitfulness of his own life would be known only after his death. Washing Peter's feet, Jesus said, "At the moment you do not know what I am doing, but later you will understand" (John 13:7).

Isn't this true of many great men and women throughout history? Many lived simple lives, some dying at a very young age. Some were barely known during their lives, or may have been known for completely different reasons than what they are remembered for. Francis of Assisi, Teresa of Avila, Vincent van Gogh, Wolfgang Amadeus Mozart, Dorothy Day, Martin Luther King, Jr., and countless others. The meaning of their lives did not become clear until long after they were gone. Decades and even centuries later we still read their books and listen to their music; we appreciate their artwork and pray their prayers; we sing their songs and aspire to their virtues. Even the life of Henri J. M. Nouwen, which ended in 1996, continues to bear fruit around the world in ways he probably never imagined when he lived. The writing of his book *Our Greatest Gift* was in response to a question he shared with his friends Nathan and Sue at dinner one evening, after Moe's funeral. When Nathan asked Henri, "Where and how do you want to die?" it raised a whole series of questions for him to ponder.

> It was a question that came from our new awareness that, like Moe, we would soon die. Our awareness prompted us to ask ourselves: Are we preparing ourselves for our death, or are we ignoring death by keeping busy? Are we helping each other to die, or do we simply assume we are going to always be there for each other? Will our death give new life, new hope, and new faith to our friends, or will it be no more than another cause for sadness? The main question is not, How much will we still be able to do during the few years we have left to live? but rather, How can we prepare ourselves for our death in such a way that our dying will be a new way for us to send our and God's spirit to those whom we have loved and who have loved us?
>
> Nathan's question, "Where and how do you want to die?" brought me face-to-face with a great challenge: not only to live well, but also to die well. . . . I wanted to write about befriending my death so that it can become my best gift to the world I love so much.[39]

The fruits of Henri's reflections on befriending death and dying well continue to manifest themselves in the lives of those touched by his living and his writing. These gifts will be there for many generations to come. Henri understood his life as mission, and he has much to teach us about how to live and how to die. He believed that the task of befriending his own death was not simply to serve himself, but to serve others also. He wanted to die well, but he also wanted to help others die well too, and he hoped that his desire to embrace his own mortality would help others to embrace theirs. In trying to befriend his own death, Henri shared a story which gave him new insights to consider, and hopefully helps us do the same.

> Recently, a friend told me a story about twins talking to each other in the womb. The sister said to the brother, "I believe there is life

after birth." Her brother protested vehemently, "No, no, this is all there is. This is a dark and cozy place, and we have nothing else to do but to cling to the cord that feeds us." The little girl insisted, "There must be something else, a place with light where there is freedom to move." Still she could not convince her twin brother.

After some silence, the sister said hesitantly, "I have something else to say, and I'm afraid you won't believe that, either, but I think there is a mother." Her brother became furious. "A mother!" he shouted. "What are you talking about? I have never seen a mother, and neither have you. Who put that idea in your head? As I told you, this place is all we have. Why do you always want more? This is not such a bad place, after all. We have all we need, so let's be content."

The sister was quite overwhelmed by her brother's response and for a while didn't dare say anything more. But she couldn't let go of her thoughts, and since she had only her twin brother to speak to, she finally said, "Don't you feel these squeezes every once in a while? They're quite unpleasant and sometimes even painful." "Yes," he answered. "What's special about that?" "Well," the sister said, "I think that these squeezes are there to get us ready for another place, much more beautiful than this, where we will see our mother face-to-face. Don't you think that's exciting?" [40]

Befriending our death comes through befriending our life. Henri's reflections gave birth to contemplating his own life and death, and can help us to do the same. Seeing ourselves as God's beloved, claiming that truth through prayer and reflection to let it shape the way we live, and understanding how our lives can become even more fruitful after we die, are important elements in befriending our inevitable death. Learning to live well not only enables us to embrace our dying, it helps us prepare ourselves to die well.

Chapter Four

DYING WELL

Is death such an absolute end of all our thoughts and actions that we simply cannot face it? Or is it possible to befriend our dying gradually and live open to it, trusting that we have nothing to fear? Is it possible to prepare for our death with the same attentiveness that our parents had in preparing for our birth? Can we wait for our death as for a friend who wants to welcome us home?

Henri Nouwen, *Our Greatest Gift*

Henri uses many different themes and images throughout his writings to explore ways of looking at our living and dying, and the steps we can take in preparing well for the end of our earthly life. Not knowing how long we will live or how we will die makes it important for us to take time to reflect on our dying while we are able to do so. Even if we are presently healthy, we will no doubt face illness of some kind during our lifetime, as well as the eventual infirmities of aging. Henri's insights can help us reflect on dying, whether we are young and healthy, whether we are assisting others on their journey, or whether we are facing a more imminent death in our own lives.

The way we look at life and death ultimately affects how we live. After all, even though we may be preparing to die, we continue to live. This is not only true to understand from a spiritual perspective, but it is also noted by the Canadian Hospice

Palliative Care Association as a hallmark from which to develop standards of practice for hospice palliative care.

> Ultimately, it is hoped that instead of being seen as "care for the dying," hospice palliative care will be known as "care that aims to relieve suffering and improve quality of life throughout the illness and bereavement experience, so that patients and families can realize their full potential to live even when they are dying."[1]

RECLAIMING OUR CHILDHOOD

Nouwen wrote that the first task in preparing ourselves well for death is to become a child again. Matthew's Gospel proclaims the same message to us: "Truly I tell you, unless you change and become like children, you will never enter the kingdom of heaven" (Mt 18:3 NRSV).

The serious van accident which Henri was involved in brought him close to death. Facing emergency surgery, he was told beforehand that there was a chance he might not survive due to extensive internal bleeding.

> [A]t that particular moment, when I realized that I might die within a few hours, I experienced an enormous amount of grace—in the sense that I experienced God's love in a very intimate and personal way. . . . I suddenly realized that I was free to die . . . because in a very deep way I was safe and I was basically returning to the embrace of love out of which I came.[2]

He goes on to explain how this experience gave him a new spiritual freedom—a freedom known in seeing himself as a child of God: "whether or not I survived the surgery, I was safely held in a divine embrace and would certainly live."[3]

What Henri refers to as a second childhood also has to do with the understanding of a new dependence. This dependence begins with our birth and returns as we age or when we face our death.

For the first twenty or so years of life, we depend on our parents, teachers, and friends. Forty years later, we again become increasingly dependent. The younger we are, the more people we need so that we may live. Life is lived from dependence to dependence.

That's the mystery that God has revealed to us through Jesus, whose life was a journey from the manger to the cross. Born in complete dependence on those who surrounded him, Jesus died as the passive victim of other people's actions and decisions. His was the journey from the first to the second childhood. He came as a child and died as a child, and he lived his life so that we may claim and reclaim our own childhood and thus make our death—as he did his—into a new birth.[4]

This can be quite a new concept for us to understand, seeing our lives as being lived from "dependence to dependence." Our society speaks so loudly of the need for us to become independent that we tend to look at dependence as a weakness or a failure. We pride ourselves in striking out on our own and becoming successful without the help of anyone else. We tend to look down on those in our world who rely on assistance to live, especially financial assistance. When we suffer infirmities which require us to turn to others for care, we look at ourselves as a burden to our families or to society. We find it difficult to accept that our dignity or our "quality of life" can be maintained even as we become more dependent on others.

Henri desired that we accept our aging, our growing dependence, and our eventual death by shifting our thinking in a different direction. His message expressed an importance in facing the reality that our life has limits. In a very early book Nouwen cowrote with Walter Gaffney called *Aging*, he used the image of a wagon wheel to talk about growing old, and how this is a normal part of living which must be embraced, without being denied or hidden.

The wagon wheel reminds us that the pains of growing old are worthwhile. The wheel turns from ground to ground, but not without moving forward. Although we have only one life cycle to live, although it is only a small part of human history which we will cover, to do this gracefully and carefully is our greatest vocation. Indeed we go from dust to dust, we move up to go down, we grow to die, but the first dust does not have to be the same as the second, the going down can become the moving on, and death can be made into our final gift.

Aging is the turning of the wheel, the gradual fulfillment of the life cycle in which receiving matures in giving and living makes dying worthwhile. Aging does not need to be hidden or denied, but can be understood, affirmed, and experienced as a process of growth by which the mystery of life is slowly revealed to us.[5]

However, instead of facing our aging gracefully, the messages in society today call us to embrace a myriad of anti-aging creams and cures, or endless types of skin treatments and plastic surgery, all in order to seek a more youthful appearance and supposedly "fulfilling" life. There is often a seeming embarrassment by many older people to shun public appearances after acquiring a disfigurement or obvious disability. This might include some form of paralysis, resulting from a cerebrovascular accident (stroke), or be associated with a visibly debilitating disease such as Parkinson's or multiple sclerosis. Perhaps no one in this generation showed us the dignity inherent in accepting their aging and physical changes publicly better than Pope John Paul II. He was a wonderful example to all of us for the need to accept and embrace our eventual infirmities, and not let them stop us from "living." This ideal is captured beautifully in a recent story told by Sister Sue Mosteller, a friend of Henri's, about an aging sister in her community.

One of the sisters in my Congregation who taught me more than fifty years ago is now one hundred years old. Today she is blind and in a wheelchair. Whenever I see her at dinner, she is not too interested in the tiny serving of food on her plate, but she is totally engaged in conversation with others at the table. Her questions are penetrating, and she loves a stimulating conversation. When newscasters came to the convent to interview her after Pope John Paul II died, they asked her to pretend to be saying her rosary and to look sad. She indignantly replied, "I'm sorry, but I talk to the Lord in a different way today! And why would I look sad that the Pope died? Didn't he lead an adventuresome life? Wasn't he amazing—the way he lived his public life to the end in such fragility? Isn't he an example of living fully and dying in his time? No, sir, I cannot put on a sad face. I feel so joyful that his mission is accomplished!"[6]

In an interview for *Cross Point Magazine,* Henri reflected similarly on aging and on dying:

As we age, the issue of our own death is something that we all must deal with. How we face the question is not as important as is the willingness to raise the question in the first place. I mean, is death an issue at all? I think for most people it is not. Most people are not at all thinking about the fruitfulness of life after death. More likely they are saying to themselves, "How can I live longer? My life is becoming less and less productive; I can do less and less and I might gradually become a burden to those around me." For some people the thought of having to be cared for is almost more than they can bear.

. . . Very few people, if any, are thinking that their death can be a good thing in the sense that Jesus meant it. That is not part of our cultural thinking, nor is it really part of the church's thinking. When the church speaks about death, it is often about the hereafter—about heaven or hell, or about another life, everlasting life and so on. That is crucial, of course, and I am not saying that it shouldn't be an important part of our thinking. I'm only saying that when people think about death, they think most often about where they are going, where they will finally end up, what there is, if anything, to look forward to. But Jesus saw death, His own death in particular, as more than a way of getting from one place to another. He saw it as potentially fruitful in itself, and of benefit to His disciples. Very few people think about death in the way Jesus thought about it.[7]

RECOGNIZING OUR FRUITFULNESS

Nouwen explains again how this element of fruitfulness can be the way in which we approach not only our living but also our dying. "The real question, then, as I consider my own death, is not: how much can I still accomplish before I die, or how many things can I still do? But the real question is: how can I prepare myself for my death in such a way that my death can bear fruit for others?"[8]

Because our culture measures the value of the human person by degrees of success, Nouwen asks us to shift our thinking from gauging our worth and our life by successfulness to fruitfulness. He looks at infirmity and aging and explains, "You can't do certain things any more and you begin to feel more dependent, weaker and more vulnerable. The challenge is to look at that vulnerability, not as a negative thing but as a positive thing—to look at it as a place where you can become fruitful."[9]

It's very interesting: fruits are always the result of vulnerability. A child is conceived when two people are vulnerable with each other in their intimacy. Or the experience of peace and reconciliation can come when people are very honest and compassionate with one another, when they are vulnerable and open about their own needs and weaknesses. . . . Then you can say, "Alright, I am weaker and more vulnerable, but perhaps this can be a good thing. For instance, I depend more on people—people have to care for me because I am physically weak. Is that really so bad?" Well, it is bad if you think in terms of success but it might just be that others can be blessed and enriched in their lives by caring for me. In this way, my weakness becomes fruitful—I am still giving something. And by gratefully receiving someone else's care, I may be allowing them to discover something of their own gift, and of the beauty of love and service.[10]

In my own life, I can profess that to be so true. Being a nurse for almost thirty years, it has been through the experiences of those who have been vulnerable and ill, many of them in various stages of dying, that I have come to know the beauty of love and service. Tending to the needs of patients, as well as personal friends and family members as they lay dying, has helped me to see the beauty of life as well as the peace and joy that can come with letting go. There is an enormous sense of sacredness and honor in having been given the opportunity to journey with the dying and their families during this precious time.

One instance in particular, which will always remain dear to my heart, was the death of my former pastor and good friend, Father Stanley McGuire. He was a very intelligent and normally independent man, who, besides being a priest for close to fifty years, had also been a university professor. He loved good books and literature, as well as a glass or two of good Scotch, and was well known as a great preacher and public speaker.

The illness that took his life came on suddenly, and he became immediately dependent on others to care for him and make decisions. You might say the journey to his second childhood was swift. With very few family members available, a host of friends, parishioners, and brother priests assisted in keeping vigil at his bedside during the ten days prior to his death. Those days were filled with many stories, as well as laughter and tears. He seemed to deteriorate on Holy Thursday, only to herald a bit of a "resurrection" Easter Sunday and awaken with an Irish gleam in his eye and a few chuckles for us all. This epiphany was short-lived, however, and he died peacefully a few days later.

Keeping him company, playing quiet music for him, anointing his tired body with lotion and his parched lips with balm were ways for these friends to serve the one who had served them for so many years. I was touched deeply by so much that happened during those days. One of the many gifts Stan gave to us was given to the parishioner who was with him when he died. Never having been present with someone when they died, she experienced what that moment meant. She was not aware at that time that she would accompany her husband on his own journey through death a few years later. Father Stan's death had borne a fruitfulness for her in experiencing that the fear of the unknown during the moment of death could surely be accompanied by peace and grace. In fact, the fruits of Stan's death were experienced most profoundly through what was his second childhood, that total dependence on his Lord, and on all of the caregivers whose lives became blessed and enriched. They, too, discovered the beauty of love and service.

LIVING OUR LOSSES

Another idea Henri explored in his writings, which helps us in exploring our own dying, is how we are called to discover life as a series of passages.

> When you are born, you leave your mother's womb, and you move to something new. When you go to school, you lose the family in a way and discover new life. When you grow old, you lose your job. Every time, the question is, can you choose to make these losses, these endless losses of your life as passages to something new? Can you choose to live your losses, not as ways to resentment, but as ways to freedom?[11]

In this sense, Nouwen looks at life as a school from which we are trained to depart. Even more than that, he looks at it as the main condition for Christian growth. If we truly learn to "live our losses" and celebrate what they can bring for us, then each encounter of departure can become a means for us to experience a growing sense of freedom.

> When we leave the safe body of our mother we are ready to breathe on our own and to start on the road to self-hood. When we depart from the close center of the family where we are the center of attention, and go to school, we have the chance to test our potentialities and develop new friendships. When we leave home to go to college we receive the freedom to re-evaluate the many things given to us and integrate what we consider as meaningful. When we leave our parents to marry or enter religious life we can experience the challenge to build our own home and to give life to others. And when we retire from our work we may have the long delayed possibility to come to terms with some of the basic dimensions of life.
>
> And if life then is a constant departure, a constant dying away from the past, to reach more independence, more freedom and more truth, why shouldn't our final departure give us the final independence, freedom, and truth for which we have been groping throughout our entire lives?[12]

It may be a new concept for us to understand our life as a series of losses, but I am sure all of us can easily recall some of the great losses in our life and remember the pain they caused us. Think back to some of your own great losses. How did you deal with them? Were you able to grow and move forward, or are you still held captive by the pain and resentment they brought into your life? Losing a loved one, losing one's health, losing a relationship or a child—none of us is spared the experience of loss in our life. Nouwen speaks about the need not only to name these losses, but to actively mourn them.

True healing begins at the moment that we can face the reality of our losses and let go of the illusions of control. Since we are such fearful people, this is the hardest challenge we face: the challenge to go beyond our fears and to trust that our losses liberate us from the bonds that hold us captive. I don't think we can do this by relying solely on our intellectual and emotional abilities. Everything in us protests against dying—in whatever form it presents itself to us. If our own human capacities are our sole resources, then it would seem that the only reasonable response to our losses would be some form of stoicism. But I do believe that the Spirit of Jesus, the Spirit of love, is given to us to reach out beyond our fears and embrace the reality of our losses. This is what mourning is all about: allowing the pain of our losses to enter our hearts; the courage to allow our wounds to be known to ourselves and felt by ourselves; the freedom to cry in anguish, or to scream in protest over our losses, and so to risk being led into an inner space that is very unfamiliar to us.[13]

Mourning is painful and often seems to be done in isolation. Healing begins when we find the courage to take our pain out of its isolation and bring it into the open. When we name it and share it, not only is it easier to bear, but we come to realize that we suffer in communion with all of humanity. Henri knew this from his own lived experience. "It was during a time of great emotional pain that I first came to L'Arche. When I saw the enormous suffering of the mentally handicapped people living there, I came gradually to see that my painful problems were part of a much larger suffering, and I found in myself new energy to live it."[14]

Being able to not only recognize our losses, but to share them and to join them to the losses of others is what gives us strength to go on. This is one important way we learn to "live" our losses. Connecting our pain to the pain of others is how we will discover the grace-filled moments that breathe new life into our suffering. Henri believed this and talked about it in many of his writ-

ings. In his diary *The Road to Daybreak* he reflects on this premise after a Good Friday liturgy he attended with the L'Arche Community in Trosly, France.

> Good Friday: day of the cross, day of suffering, day of hope, day of abandonment, day of victory, day of mourning, day of joy, day of endings, day of beginnings.
>
> During the liturgy, . . . Père [Father] Thomas and Père [Father] Gilbert . . . took the huge cross that hangs behind the altar from the wall and held it so that the whole community could come and kiss the dead body of Christ.
>
> They all came, more than four hundred people—handicapped men and women and their assistants and friends. Everybody seemed to know very well what they were doing: expressing their love and gratitude for him who gave his life for them. As they were crowding around the cross and kissing the feet and the head of Jesus, I closed my eyes and could see his sacred body stretched out and crucified upon our planet earth. I saw the immense suffering of humanity during the centuries: people killing each other; people dying from starvation and epidemics; people driven from their homes; people sleeping on the streets of large cities; people clinging to each other in desperation; people flagellated, tortured, burned, and mutilated; people alone in locked flats, in prison dungeons, in labor camps; people craving a gentle word, a friendly letter, a consoling embrace; people—children, teenagers, adults, middle-aged, and elderly—all crying out with an anguished voice: "My God, my God, why have you forsaken us?"
>
> Imagining the naked, lacerated body of Christ stretched out over our globe, I was filled with horror. But as I opened my eyes I saw Jacques, who bears the marks of suffering in his face, kiss the body with passion and tears in his eyes. I saw Ivan carried on Michael's back. I saw Edith coming in her wheelchair. As they came—walking or limping, seeing or blind, hearing or deaf—I saw the endless procession of humanity gathering around the sacred

body of Jesus, covering it with their tears and their kisses, and slowly moving away from it comforted and consoled by such great love. There were signs of relief; there were smiles breaking through tear-filled eyes; there were hands in hands and arms in arms. With my mind's eye I saw the huge crowds of isolated, agonizing individuals walking away from the cross together, bound by the love they had seen with their own eyes and touched with their own lips. The cross of horror became the cross of hope; the tortured body became the body that gives new life; the gaping wounds became the source of forgiveness, healing and reconciliation.[15]

It is so easy during times of struggle and pain, to give up hope. We are tempted to respond with the sense that God has not heard our prayers, that indeed God has abandoned us. We find ourselves asking so many questions. How can a God of love allow so much suffering? Why is there no cure for this illness? Why doesn't this God answer our prayers?

Henri reflected on this sense of hopelessness when he was living at the Abbey of the Genesee.

The world in which we live today and about whose suffering we know so much seems more than ever a world from which Christ has withdrawn himself. How can we believe that in this world, we are constantly being prepared to receive the Spirit? Still, I think that this is exactly the message of hope. God has not withdrawn himself. He sent his Son to share our human condition and the Son sent us his Spirit to lead us into the intimacy of his divine life. It is in the midst of the chaotic suffering of humanity that the Holy Spirit, the Spirit of Love, makes himself visible. But can we recognize his presence?[16]

If we open our eyes and hearts, we will recognize the presence of the Spirit in many ways. We see it through the gift of the presence of others who walk with us on our journey; through the gift

of peacefulness felt in our hearts during times of chaos; through the gift of caregivers who offer us compassion and healing; through the gift of reconciliation that is often revealed when lost friends and family members find one another again. In these and countless other ways, we are made aware of the presence of God in our midst, and the Spirit of healing in our pain. Understanding the love and presence of the Spirit in this way helps us with another often misunderstood concept about suffering.

> We are often tempted to "explain" suffering in terms of "the will of God." Not only can this evoke anger and frustration, but also it is false. "God's will" is not a label that can be put on unhappy situations. God wants to bring joy not pain, peace not war, healing not suffering. Therefore, instead of declaring anything and everything to be the will of God, we must be willing to ask ourselves where in the midst of our pains and sufferings we can discern the loving presence of God.[17]

Recognizing or discerning the loving presence of God can only be done if we try to stay connected to God through raising our awareness of how God is already at work in our lives. Raising our awareness can happen when we take time for solitude and prayer. During these times, we can reflect on our day and notice where God was present in the events and conversations that unfolded. When did I experience joy? Love? Acceptance? Peace? Learning to recognize and celebrate these encounters is so important in being able to trust that God will continue to love us and provide for whatever we need. Once we trust more and more in the presence and love of God, we can start to let go of the illusion of control which we try to hold on to so tightly. We will start to live in the present, and celebrate today, worrying less about tomorrow.

> When I trust deeply that today God is truly with me and holds me safe in a divine embrace, guiding every one of my steps, I can let

go of my anxious need to know how tomorrow will look, or what will happen next month or next year. I can be fully where I am and pay attention to the many signs of God's love within and around me.[18]

Learning how to claim our identity as God's children, with complete trust in God's love for us, helps us endure the pain of living the losses of our life. Understanding the importance of naming and mourning these losses helps us continue to live fully, even as we face our death. However, the same Spirit of healing that calls us to mourn, also calls us to dance!

TURNING OUR MOURNING INTO DANCING

Mourning our losses can create an inner emptiness and bring us in touch with our nothingness. Mourning makes us poor, but it is in that nothingness, in that poverty and emptiness, that we can begin to rise up.

The Spirit of healing that makes us mourn is the same Spirit that makes us dance. The dance does not begin after all the grief is over. The dance finds its origin in the grieving itself. . . . "Blessed are those who mourn." Jesus does not say, "Blessed are those who console the mourner." No, he says, "You are blessed in your mourning." There is the place where the Spirit brings you new life. There is the crèche where the Child is born in you. There is the broken soil of your soul where the seed of grace can grow in you. . . . [T]he Spirit of Jesus says: "Your glory is hidden in your pain."[19]

Once you have been stripped naked, you have found a new freedom. There is nothing to inhibit your movement anymore.

Can you notice in your innermost being the joy of living that comes from having nothing left to lose? Can you see the soft, beautiful smile that appears in the tearful eyes of your mourning friend? Jesus enters into our sadness, takes us by the hand, pulls us gently up to where we can stand, and invites us to dance. And as we dance, we realize that we don't have to stay on the little spot of our grief, but can step beyond it into unknown, spacious territory until we finally know that all the world is our dance floor.[20]

Henri illustrates this with a wonderful reflection sent to him by a good friend.

My friend had decided to spend the week following Christmas with his father who suffers from Alzheimer's Disease. One morning, when he met his father at the day program in which he takes part, he found him very anxious and agitated. His father was worrying that his own mother, who had died long before my friend was born, needed his help. The worries were clearly an expression of a deep anguish that couldn't be expressed directly. My friend took his father for a drive for more than an hour through the countryside. Very few words were spoken between them, but my friend noticed how his father's anxiety diminished and he became more relaxed. After not speaking for nearly an hour, the father turned, looked directly at his son, and said: "Well, we haven't had such a good visit in a long time." The son laughed and realized that his father was right. Anguish had become peace; sadness had become gladness; loss had become gain; mourning had become dancing.[21]

In trying to conceptualize the image of this dance, Nouwen breaks it down for us into two movements. Being able to move out of our mourning and to dance again in the dance of life calls for us to begin by taking the first step, which is "forgiveness." For many people, this can be a very difficult step to take, but one that is essential if we are to be able to move on to the second movement of "celebration." There is the need to forgive our parents, for the times they were unable to love us completely, and our siblings and friends for not being there for us when we needed them. Beyond that, we have to forgive the failings of our civic leaders, of our church, and even forgive all those who torture, kill, and destroy, making the world a darker place. We also have to beg forgiveness for ourselves, for the times we have failed others as well as our society. It is always difficult to forgive and to ask for forgiveness, but if we do not, we will remain victims of our past, "chained to our personal and communal history by guilt and shame—unable to dance."[22]

As mentioned earlier, Henri was involved in a serious van accident which warranted emergency surgery. Before his operation, and knowing that he might not pull through, he experienced warmth, a love, and an acceptance that he had never experienced before. He knew that he was ready to face death. However, upon waking from the surgery, and realizing that he had not died, he was filled with confusion. He wondered why he wasn't "good enough" for God to take him home at that moment. He eventually came to realize that he was not ready to let go of his life until he addressed some outstanding issues of forgiveness.

What most prevented me from dying was the sense of unfinished business, unresolved conflicts with people with whom I live or had lived. The pain of forgiveness withheld, by me and from me, kept me clinging to my wounded existence. In my mind's eye, I saw the men and women who aroused within me feelings of anger, jealousy and even hatred. They had a strange power over me. They might never think of me, but every time I thought of them I lost some of my inner peace and joy. Their criticism, rejection or expressions of personal dislike still affected my feelings about myself. By not truly forgiving them from the heart, I gave them a power over me that kept me chained to my old, broken existence. I also knew that there were still people angry with me, people who could not think about me or speak about me without experiencing great hostility. I might not even know what I had done or said to them. I might not even know who they were. They had not forgiven me, but held on to me in their anger.

In the face of death, I realized that it was not love that kept me clinging to life, but unresolved anger. . . .

As I felt life weakening in me, I felt a deep desire to forgive and to be forgiven, to let go of all evaluations and opinions, to be free from the burden of judgements. I said to Sue, "Please tell everyone who has hurt me that I have forgiven them from my heart, and please ask everyone whom I have hurt to forgive me too.". . .

What worried me most during these hours was that my death might make someone feel guilty, ashamed or left hanging spiritually in mid-air. I was afraid that someone would say or think: "I wish there had been a chance to resolve our conflict, to say what I really feel, to express my true intentions. . . . I wish, but now it is too late." I know how hard it is to live with these unsaid words and withheld gestures. They can deepen our darkness and become a burden of guilt.[23]

This reflection strongly reminds us of the power of forgiveness. So often, a large part of being able to die well, and to move forward with no regrets, is to be able to make amends with those we have been estranged from. We all know people for whom this has been the case. There are stories of joy where forgiveness was given or received and stories of pain where it has been absent. However, we should not postpone this task until we are dying in order to make amends and experience forgiveness. On the contrary, seeking forgiveness as issues arise will allow us to live our lives in freedom as the children of God.

Death often happens suddenly. A car accident, a plane crash, a fatal fight, a war, a flood, and so on. When we feel healthy and full of energy, we do not think much about our death. Still, death might come very unexpectedly.

How can we be prepared to die? By not having any unfinished relational business. The question is, Have I forgiven those who have

hurt me and asked forgiveness from those I have hurt? When I feel
at peace with all the people who are part of my life, my death
might cause great grief, but it will not cause guilt or anger.

When we are ready to die at any moment, we are also ready
to live at any moment.[24]

In order for us to be able to turn our mourning into dancing
and dance in freedom, we must be at peace with the people who
are a part of our lives. Only after dancing the first movement of
forgiveness, can we go on to the second. In the second movement, we are called to dance freely, the dance of celebration! No
matter how strong or fragile our bodies may be, if we are able to
claim our belovedness and embrace our life in gratitude, we can
continue living and celebrating even when we are dying.

There is nothing as healing as celebrating life in this way. Our call to
be healers is a call to claim the new life that bursts forth from our
mourning and to let that new life take us far beyond the boundaries
of our mortality. This is the true secret of celebration: the life we celebrate is not imprisoned within the boundaries of birth and death;
it is not caught in the fatalism of our chronology; it is not based on
the little bits of happiness with which our world tempts us, such as
success, popularity or power. No, the life we celebrate is the life of
the Spirit within us. It is the life that existed before we were born
and will exist after we have died. It is the life of God given to us from
all eternity to all eternity. . . . Celebration is so healing because it lifts
up the truth that we do not belong to the restricting, limiting and
destructive power of our world, but to God whose name is life and
love, and who holds us safe even when the power of sickness and
death seems to take everything away from us.[25]

Henri reflects on this notion of celebration in the September
8 entry in his diary *The Road to Daybreak*. He occasionally corre-
sponded with an English doctor Sheila Cassidy, who had been

imprisoned and tortured two years after General Pinochet took power in Chile. Although they had never met, their lives touched each other's through their writings. Here he shares a short description she sent to him of a hospice, followed by his own thoughts which were penned in the diary that day.

Medically speaking, hospices exist to provide a service of pain and symptom control for those for whom active anti-cancer treatment is no longer appropriate—there is always something that can be done for the dying, even if it's only having the patience and courage to sit with them. Most lay people imagine that hospices are solemn, rather depressing places where voices are hushed and eyes downcast as patients and their families await the inevitable. Nothing could be further from the truth. Hospice care is about life and love and laughter, for it is founded upon two unshakable beliefs: that life is so precious that each minute should be lived to the full, and that death is quite simply a part of life, to be faced openly and greeted with the hand outstretched. One of the hallmarks of hospice life is celebration: cakes are baked and champagne uncorked at the first hint of a birthday or anniversary, and administrators, nurses, and volunteers clink glasses with patients and their families.

As I read this, I was struck that much, if not all, that Sheila Cassidy says can be said of L'Arche as well. A hospice is for the dying who cannot be cured of their disease; L'Arche is for the handicapped whose handicap cannot be removed. Both proclaim loudly the preciousness of life and encourage us to face reality with open eyes and outstretched hands. Both are places of celebration in which the certainty of the present is always much more important than the uncertainty of the future. Both are witnesses to the paradox that the most unlikely people are chosen by God to make us see. Sheila Cassidy and Jean Vanier found their vocations in very different ways, but their common faith in Jesus and his Gospel has given them a remarkably similar vision.[26]

"That is why Mother Teresa and Jean Vanier consider joy the main characteristic of those who walk among the dying and the disabled. Their joy comes from that deep-rooted knowledge that, . . . we, yes, you and I, truly belong to the God whose name is love and who showed us that love in the total vulnerability of Jesus."[27]

In order for us to dance the dance of celebration, we must learn to sing the song of gratitude. If we can look at everything that is given to us as being gift, if we can live and be grateful for all of our experiences and see the fruitfulness that comes forth from them, we can dance the dance of celebration. It will no longer matter what we do or where we are—all will become a part of the dance. Our working and resting, our eating and drinking, and our encounters with others, will all become an invitation to celebrate—an invitation to dance in gratitude!

Along with trust there must be gratitude—the opposite of resentment. Resentment and gratitude cannot coexist, since resentment blocks the perception and experience of life as a gift. My resentment tells me that I don't receive what I deserve. It always manifests itself in envy.

Gratitude, however, goes beyond the "mine" and "thine" and claims the truth that all of life is a pure gift. In the past I always thought of gratitude as a spontaneous response to the awareness of gifts received, but now I realize that gratitude can also be lived as a discipline. The discipline of gratitude is the explicit effort to acknowledge that all I am and have is given to me as a gift of love, a gift to be celebrated in joy.

Gratitude as a discipline involves a conscious choice. I can choose to be grateful even when my emotions and feelings are still steeped in hurt and resentment. It is amazing how many occasions present themselves in which I can choose gratitude instead of a complaint . . . .

There is always the choice between resentment and gratitude because God has appeared in my darkness, urged me to come home, and declared in a voice filled with affection: "You are with

me always, and all I have is yours." Indeed, I can choose to dwell
in the darkness in which I stand, point to those who are seemingly better off than I, lament about the many misfortunes that have
plagued me in the past, and thereby wrap myself up in my resentment. But I don't have to do this. There is the option to look into
the eyes of the One who came out to search for me and see there-
in that all I am and all I have is pure gift calling for gratitude.[28]

In looking closer at gratefulness and dying well, Nouwen
explains the connection for us even more clearly.

When we think about death, we often think about what will happen to us after we have died. But it is more important to think
about what will happen to those we leave behind. The way we die
has a deep and lasting effect on those who stay alive. It will be easier for our family and friends to remember us with joy and peace if
we have said a grateful good-bye than if we die with bitter and dis-
illusioned hearts.
    The greatest gift we can offer our families and friends is the
gift of gratitude. Gratitude sets them free to continue living without bitterness or self-recrimination.[29]

However, just as anyone who is learning to dance can attest,
dancing calls for discipline. In order to dance well, one has to
enroll in dancing school. Dancing is hard work, and discipleship
without discipline is like wanting to follow the great Dancer without ever being willing to practice. For that reason, we know one
thing is for certain:

The dance, beautiful as it may look to the outsider, is always the
fruit of long training and much sweat and tears. And there will be
many moments of great spiritual fatigue; yes, even despair, with
our heads down, our hair unkempt, our bodies bowed down to the
floor, and no movement at all. Jesus lived such moments in the

Garden of Gethsemane when he cried out: "Father, if it is possible, let this cup pass by me." Only now can we say that even that moment was part of the dance. When we live it, however, it seems that all is lost. We will always need someone, a therapist, a counselor, a friend, a lover, who can encourage us to remain faithful to our self-chosen disciplines and to remind us over and over again that what we experience as complete failure and complete regression is, in fact, part of the spiritual choreography of our lives. This encouragement and this reminding are an essential element of all healing in and through the Spirit.

And notice: You are not dancing alone. There are many dancers on the floor. Keep aware of their presence. When you are ready to move, trust that those who seem immobile are part of the larger performance, and, when you lie prostrate on the floor, trust that those who fly around you in graceful motion, receive admiration because your depression transforms their ecstasy into true art. We are all together on the stage of life, and God, with a tear and with a smile, looks with favor on his children.[30]

Understanding that we are not dancing alone gives us the courage and strength we need to go on. It allows us to see the presence of the others as pure gift. Gratitude results from recognizing that all that is, is a divine gift, born out of love and freely given, so that we may offer thanks and share it with others. One of the most moving stories about gratitude is told by the Evangelist John, about the multiplication of loaves and fishes. This story, found in John 6:5–15, is broken open by Henri for us.

When Jesus saw the hungry crowds and wondered where to buy some bread for the people to eat, Andrew said: "There is a small boy here with five barley loaves and two fish; but what is that for so many?" Andrew's word powerfully summarizes our attitude as fearful people. The needs are enormous, the reserves are small, so what can we do? The implication of this attitude is clearly: let us hold on to the little we have so that we at least survive. But "Jesus took the loaves, gave thanks, and gave them out to all who were sitting ready; he then did the same with the fish, giving out as much as was wanted." This radical shift of vision, from looking at the loaves and fishes as scarce products which need to be hoarded, to seeing them as precious gifts from God which ask to be gratefully shared, is the movement from wreaking death to bringing forth life, the movement from fear to love.[31]

MOVING FROM FEAR TO LOVE

Another important movement in the dance of living, or dying, is the movement from fear to love. As long as we are afraid, it is not only difficult for us to live well and love well, but it is also difficult for us to die well.

We are a fearful people. We are afraid of conflict, war, an uncertain future, illness, and, most of all, death. This fear takes away our freedom and gives our society the power to manipulate us with threats and promises. When we can reach beyond our fears to the One who loves us with a love that was there before we were born and will be there after we die, then oppression, persecution, and even death will be unable to take our freedom. Once we have come to the deep inner knowledge—a knowledge more of the heart than of the mind—that we are born out of love and will die into love, that every part of our being is deeply rooted in love and that this love is our true Father and Mother, then all forms of evil, illness, and death lose their final power over us and become painful but hopeful reminders of our true divine childhood. The apostle Paul expressed this experience of the complete freedom of the children of God when he wrote, "I am certain of this: neither death nor life, nor angels, nor principalities, nothing already in existence and nothing still to come, nor any power, nor the heights nor the depths, nor any created thing whatever, will be able to come between us and the love of God, known to us in Christ Jesus" (Romans 8:38–39).[32]

Letting go of our fears and trusting completely in the love of God seems to be the most difficult step to take in our movement toward dying well. Who of us is not afraid to die? Who is really not afraid of the pain or the unknown? Even with a tremendous amount of faith it is difficult to surrender totally not only our hearts, minds, and souls, but our bodies as well.

Nouwen reflects about fear and love in his journal *The Inner Voice of Love*. This book was written at a time in Henri's life when he was very shattered and broken, and undergoing therapy for a psychological crisis in his life. During this time, he reaches some profound insights, which he courageously shares with readers through his journal entries. This one is titled "Claim the Victory."

You are still afraid to die. That fear is connected with the fear that you are not loved. Your question "Do you love me?" and your question "Do I have to die?" are deeply connected. You asked these questions as a little child, and you are still asking them.

As you come to know that you are loved fully and unconditionally, you will also come to know that you do not have to fear death. Love is stronger than death; God's love was there for you before you were born and will be there for you after you have died.

Jesus has called you from the moment you were knitted together in your mother's womb. It is your vocation to receive and give love. But from the very beginning you have experienced the forces of death. They attacked you all through your years of growing up. You have been faithful to your vocation even though you have often felt overwhelmed by darkness. You know now that these dark forces will have no final power over you. He overcame for you the power of death so that you could live in freedom.

You have to claim that victory and not live as if death still controlled you. Your soul knows about the victory, but your mind and emotions have not fully accepted it. They go on struggling. In this respect you remain a person of little faith. Trust the victory and let your mind and emotions gradually be converted to the truth. You will experience new joy and new peace as you let that truth reach every part of your being. Don't forget: victory has been won, the powers of darkness no longer rule, love is stronger than death.[33]

Again, we are able to see that the single most important factor in our spiritual journey, our journey through living and dying, is believing wholeheartedly that our God is a God who loves us completely, unconditionally, and totally. Our God loves us with a perfect love—which is something we as humans cannot fathom or attain in our humanity. Only in divinity is this possible. Our whole earthly lives are spent learning lessons about what love is and how to love more completely and totally. Yet, we will never reach that potential of perfect love, until we are united with our God and Creator, the One who has loved us with that "first love."

God is our loving parent in whom nothing that is not love can be found. Apprehension, fear, and anxiety cannot sustain themselves in God's presence. Fear always creates distance and divisions. But in the presence of God fear melts away. "In love there can be no fear, but fear is driven out by perfect love" (1 Jn 4:18).

Thus, when we pay careful attention to the living presence of God, the suffering to which we might be led will never darken our hearts or paralyze our movements. We will find that we will never be asked to suffer more than we can bear and never be tested beyond our strength. When we are led by love instead of driven by fear, we can enter the places of the greatest darkness and pain and experience in a unique way the power of God's care. Jesus' final words to Peter are the strongest affirmation of this truth. After having asked Peter three times, "Do you love me?" and after having been assured three times by Peter of his love, Jesus said, "When you grow old you will stretch out your hands, and somebody else will put a belt around you and take you where you would rather not go" (Jn 21:18). Although Peter did not desire it, he was led to the cross as Jesus was. But because it was love and not fear that led him there, the cross was no longer a sign of defeat, but a sign of victory.[34]

In another one of Nouwen's spiritual classics, *The Return of the Prodigal Son*, he speaks more about this perfect love that the Father has for us. Gazing on Rembrandt's painting of the Prodigal Son, which was the inspiration for this work, Henri reflects first on assuming the role of the Prodigal Son who is returning home, then reflects on the person of the brother, and finally on the person of the Father. In the Gospel parable of the same name, found in Luke 15:11–32, we know Jesus is referring to his own Father and the kind of love he evokes, which is perfect love.

Rembrandt's painting and his own tragic life have offered me a context in which to discover that the final stage of the spiritual life is to so fully let go of all fear of the Father that it becomes possible to become like him. As long as the Father evokes fear, he remains an outsider and cannot dwell within me. But Rembrandt, who showed me the Father in utmost vulnerability, made me come to the awareness that my final vocation is indeed to become like the Father and to live out his divine compassion in my daily life. Though I am both the younger son and the elder son, I am not to remain them, but to become the Father. No father or mother ever became father or mother without having been son or daughter, but every son and daughter has to consciously choose to step beyond their childhood and become father and mother for others. It is a hard and lonely step to take—especially in a period of history in which parenthood is so hard to live well—but it is a step that is essential for the fulfillment of the spiritual journey.[35]

Being able to truly move from living in fear of God, to living in love with God, from living in fear of dying, to living in anticipation of the fruitfulness that our life will continue to bear will help us not only to live well but also to die well. This, no doubt, seems difficult, if not impossible, although we know that everything is possible where God's energy or grace is tapped into. "Just as the branch cannot bear fruit by itself unless it abides in the vine, neither can you unless you abide in me. Those who abide in me and I in them bear much fruit, because apart from me you can do nothing. . . . I have said these things to you so that my joy may be in you, and that your joy may be complete" (Jn 15:4–5, 11 NRSV).

Perhaps it will help us begin to let go of our fears by looking at an image of letting go in surrender and faith which is a little more lighthearted and tangible. One of the things that Henri became fascinated with the last five years of his life was the trapeze. He went to a circus performance in Germany with his father in 1991 and was instantly enthralled by a trapeze act from South Africa called the Flying Rodleighs. Over the next few years, he went back to see them time and again, even joining them for practices, and eventually arranging to follow their act from city to city and live in a trailer the way they did. There were many things that drew him to their act, and compelled him to want to write a book about what they did. The book was never written before he died, but he did record a video with them in 1995 entitled *Angels over the Net*. In it, he speaks about what this fascination meant to him:

> To me it was much more than an act—a show—it was a picture of life. What happened in ten minutes was really a result of a lifetime of work, of commitment, of enthusiasm, of thinking, of working—it fascinated me and I wanted to grab it from the inside. . . .
>
> The trapeze artists are people who don't speak, yet they do something with their bodies and create community—with one

another and with those who come to see them. Young, old, differ-ent languages, all understand them. They create community wher-ever they go. . . .

[Rodleigh Stevens, the flyer in the act, tells Henri:] "Everybody always says that the great hero of the trapeze is the flyer. I'm the flyer, and I make all the tricks and somersaults and people applaud and think I'm great. But the real hero is the catcher. I can only fly freely when I know that the catcher is going to catch me; when I know that when I come back from my trip [through the air], some-one will grab me." . . .

[Henri:] . . . That's what life is all about. We want to fly freely in the air of life, but we have to know that when we come down from it all we're going to be caught and be safe. We have to trust the catcher![36]

For Henri, this notion became the cornerstone of his living! It was the tangible image that illustrated for him how to move from fear to love. All he had to do was trust the catcher! All he had to do was trust God, with a complete trust, free from all fear. Then, he knew when it was time for him to return home, he would be caught! For the trapeze artist, the secret was to put your arms out in total trust and let the catcher catch you. If you har-bored any fear and tried to grab the catcher's wrists, you could break them, or break your own, falling into the dark. For that rea-son, it was essential to trust the catcher totally, fully and fearless-ly extending your arms, assured of being caught and carried to safety each time.

BELIEVING THAT WE DO NOT DIE ALONE

When Henri spoke in Chicago at the U.S. National Catholic AIDS Network Conference in July of 1995, he spoke passionately about another element which he believed in wholeheartedly. It had to do with something he referred to as

"spiritual midwifery." Referring to his near fatal accident, he recounted:

> When I was close to death, I experienced one thing: I didn't want to be alone. It seems to me that dying is less painful than dying alone. Dying is maybe not even the great agony; it is dying alone. . . . Someone has to be my midwife into death. Just as I am not born alone, I am not going to die alone. . . . It is good to have your husband there, it is good to have your lover there, good to have your mom there, good to have your friends there. . . . But none of these individuals can finally give us the spiritual power to make that passage. My deepest conviction is that what allows us to make the passage finally is the communion of saints.[37]

I'm sure at this point in the presentation, Henri had some people wondering why he was moving in this direction. The communion of saints isn't something we speak of often in our more modern discussions on spirituality. And yet, I believe that his explanation of this doctrine, and what it means for us, is quite profound.

> "I believe in the Holy Spirit, the Holy Catholic Church, the communion of saints, the resurrection of the body, and life everlasting. . . ." I don't think that "communion of saints" has dropped out there. *We are called to reclaim that spiritual doctrine, if we want to know about the communion of saints* [emphasis his].
>
> During the Reformation, the Catholic Church was so corrupt that the "communion of saints" became associated with buying people out of purgatory. As a result, the Protestant reformation said you can't pray to the saints. The saints are justified by God, and you cannot buy and pray for them. As a result, people stopped praying for the dead. They didn't think about those who have died. They were no longer part of the family because you couldn't pray for saints. I talked to a lot of people who want to pray for those who have died but don't know how to do it. So with the

Reformation or the Counter-Reformation, we have lost a deep sense of community.

Think about the AIDS situation and the AIDS crisis. I think you and I are called to reclaim the incredible and beautiful choice of the community of saints. That means that people who have died before you and people who will die after you belong to one huge big family. You are just a small part of a much larger community that you have to grab and you have to feel. You belong to the people who went before you. You can talk about the saints like St. Francis or Benedict or Ignatius and that is important, but because you have thousands of people who went before you, they are a new family. You have to hold onto them. You have to embrace them as saints. Yes, those who were born and died long ago struggled like me and were anguished like me. They had their sexual struggles as I have, and they were lonely and depressed and confused. They went through the Black Plague. They are a part of my human family.

As far as I look back and as far as I look forward, I see this crowd of witnesses that I belong to. I am just there for a moment, but I have been there, and I will be there because of those who lived before and those who will live after me. I think the communion of saints is that incredible spiritual family that surrounds you and that makes your exodus possible.

. . . All these people who have died in your life and in my life, and more and more will, are not only a source of sorrow; they can give me the sense of longing for that family that reaches out beyond the boundaries of birth and death. That is the huge perspective that is offered to us.

I hope that somehow you and I can rediscover that hundreds of people hold us. Your body, sick or weak, is connected with bodies of people all over the world. You are held safe, not just by a god, but by a god who creates a people. You are a part of that people that travels from Egypt and the new land. You are part of the people that travels through the boundaries of life, part of the people that somehow belongs together, and you claim a communion with them.[38]

Henri goes on to explain how at L'Arche, where he lives with the Daybreak community, they believe it's important to keep celebrating someone's death and to think about them every day.

[W]e talk about the dead; we have their pictures up. Finally, I realized that Laurie, Helen and Morris, the three people in the community who died the last few years, are all there. They continue to send their spirit to me. They continue to send their love to me. They continue to tell me what life is about. The more I hold onto their memories, the more it's not just remembering someone who is gone. They are active in my gut, active in my heart, active in my life. In a way, I realize that I have been given them so that I can live and discover how to live. I need them just as they needed me when they were with me. I continue to need them, and they continue to tell me something about who I am and where I am going and to whom I belong.[39]

Henri had stated more than once, to his friends, and in his writings, that his real fear related to dying would be the thought of dying alone. The irony of this story, is that when Henri Nouwen died in the Netherlands on September 21, 1996, he died essentially alone. That is, alone, as far as his living friends or family were concerned. They had spent much time at his bedside after he suffered his initial heart attack, but since he was recuperating well and was close to being discharged, they had returned home for the night. When a second heart attack claimed his life, he was alone, except for the health care workers who tried so hard to revive him. Yet, I believe, because of what he has stated here about the communion of saints being our "spiritual midwives" through death and assisting us in our passage, that he knew he was not alone. Indeed, his own mother whom he loved so dearly was no doubt there close to his side through it all, having predeceased him many years before. Henri's years of anguish and fears were now released. I am sure he triumphantly reached forward and landed safely in the hands of his Beloved Catcher!

In *Bread for the Journey,* a book of reflections for every day, which Henri penned during what was to be the final year of his life, he speaks passionately about what he ultimately believes about our lives and about God.

> One thing we know for sure about our God: Our God is a God of the living, not of the dead. God is life. God is love. God is beauty. God is goodness. God is truth. God doesn't want us to die. God wants us to live. Our God, who loves us from eternity to eternity, wants to give us life for eternity.
>
> When that life was interrupted by our unwillingness to give our full yes to God's love, God sent Jesus to be with us and to say that great yes in our name and thus restore us to eternal life. So let's not be afraid of death. There is no cruel boss, vengeful enemy, or cruel tyrant waiting to destroy us—only a loving, always forgiving God, eager to welcome us home.[40]

Through Henri's living, his own dying, and the insights shared from his many writings, we have been given much to consider when it comes to dying well. Reclaiming our childhood, both as understanding ourselves to be children of God and as learning to see our lives as lived from "dependence to dependence," is important. Being able to measure our life's worth by fruitfulness and not success, and learning to really live the losses of our life are also important concepts. Living our losses occurs when we can recognize what they are, name them, and mourn them, but ultimately be able to turn that mourning into dancing. Dancing the dance of life well is dependent on our willingness to forgive and our ability to celebrate in gratitude, recognizing that everything we receive and experience in life is pure gift.

Celebrating freely both our living and our dying can only happen when we set aside our fears and reach out in love—not only to one another but also to our God. Moving from fear to love occurs when we are able to trust that our God loves us unconditionally and will always be there to catch us while we live, and as we die. Can we do that? Can we believe that this God, who formed us out of love, and desires only to love us and be loved in return, will carry us faithfully through both our life and our death? I hope and pray that we can. And, as our final moments approach, may we take consolation in knowing that our extended family, the communion of saints, all those we have known and not known who have gone before us, will be there as spiritual midwives, to assist us in our final passage from this world to eternity.

Chapter Five

CARING WELL

*Befriending our own death and helping others to befriend theirs are insep-
arable. In the realm of the Spirit of God, living and caring are one. . . .
[C]aring is the privilege of every person and is at the heart of being human.*
Henri Nouwen, Our Greatest Gift

All of us would like to believe that we are people who care. As
a society, we tend to use the word "care" in many ambiguous
ways. "Do you want a coffee?" "I don't care." Or, "Who will look
after the house?" "I'll take care of it." However, real care is not
ambiguous or indifferent, and it is the opposite of apathy.

> The word "care" finds its roots in the Gothic Kara, which means
> lament. The basic meaning of care is "to grieve, to experience sor-
> row, to cry out with." I am very much struck by this background of
> the word "care" because we tend to look at caring as an attitude
> of the strong toward the weak, of the powerful toward the pow-
> erless, of the have's toward the have-not's. And, in fact, we feel
> quite uncomfortable with an invitation to enter into someone's
> pain before doing something about it.[1]

Looking at the word "care" in this context brings to light a different way of responding to one who is suffering. Perhaps you
remember a time when you were called to be with a friend who had

just lost a loved one and found yourself feeling totally helpless at that moment. What is there to say? What is there to do? We are so inclined to respond with things like "Don't cry, you had a good life together," or "Don't be sad, at least they're not suffering anymore." If we were ready to truly enter into their pain and not try to "do" something about it, to experience our own powerlessness in the face of death, we might find ourselves saying instead, "I don't understand either. I don't know what to do, but I am here with you." Henri asks us, "Are we willing to *not* run away from the pain, to *not* get busy when there is nothing to do, and instead stand in the face of death together with those who grieve?"[2] He reflects further:

> Still, when we honestly ask ourselves which persons in our lives mean the most to us, we often find that it is those who, instead of giving much advice, solutions, or cures, have chosen rather to share our pain and touch our wounds with a gentle and tender hand. The friend who can be silent with us in a moment of despair or confusion, who can stay with us in an hour of grief and bereavement, who can tolerate not-knowing, not-curing, not-healing and face with us the reality of our powerlessness, that is the friend who cares.[3]

THE GIFT OF PRESENCE

Henri not only wrote about the need for sitting silently in solidarity with those who are hurting, he was a man who made himself available for others and practiced this gift of being present in countless ways. He cared about those who were weak and vulnerable, whether they were lonely or physically handicapped, or among the poor he lived with in South America. He cared about the homeless people he stopped to talk to on the streets of Toronto, as well as many of his own family or friends who were suffering or dying. Many stories abound of his ability to be truly present, and offer this gift of care to others. Certainly, he has much to teach us. Here, he reflects on an encounter with a grieving friend:

I also remember the time that a friend came to me and told me that his wife had left him that day. He sat in front of me, tears streaming from his eyes. I didn't know what to say. There simply was nothing to say. My friend didn't need words. What he needed was simply to be with a friend. I held his hands in mine, and we sat there . . . silently. For a moment, I wanted to ask him how and why it all had happened, but I knew that this was not the time for questions. It was the time just to be together as friends who have nothing to say, but are not afraid to remain silent together.

Today, when I think of that day, I feel a deep gratitude that my friend had entrusted his grief to me.

These moments of compassion continue to bear fruit.[4]

There is a wonderful book titled *Befriending Life*, which is a collection of stories and reflections written about Henri by many of his friends. They wanted a chance to share with others Henri's influence on their lives. The stories were written after he had died, and the book was published five years after his death. The stories are windows into Henri's life and ministry that help us see how Henri touched people deeply, not only through his writings, but through who he was and how he lived. Beth Porter, a friend of Henri's who edited the book, expresses what many felt about this extraordinary man.

To us at Daybreak, Henri Nouwen was friend and pastor, and his gifts were manifold—he loved us, he loved God, he loved life, and he listened well and offered us valuable spiritual insight. . . . Henri taught us to remember those who had died by telling stories about them. Henri stories abound at Daybreak and, told with humor and gratitude, they are a source of joy and wisdom.[5]

In an excerpt from a reflection written by Mary Bastedo, we see how Henri shares this gift of presence so readily and models for us the kind of caring which he so often wrote about. Mary, an occupational therapist and long-time member of L'Arche, was chair of the spiritual life committee at L'Arche Daybreak when Henri arrived in the community. In sharing her story of Henri's impact on the Daybreak community, she writes:

> Raymond Batchelor, one of the core members in the New House, was struck by a car as he tried to cross the busy highway in front of Daybreak. Henri was immediately present—to Raymond, to his family, and to the Daybreak community—bringing comfort and leading us in prayer. . . .
>
> Another key element of Henri's spirituality was intimacy. Henri always struggled with intimacy: yet he was able to achieve it, especially in his capacity to move in close to those who were suffering. We witnessed this with Raymond and his family after the car accident and we saw it repeatedly. Henri taught the community a lot about compassionate presence to those who are suffering and, especially, to those who are dying. All that we learned was preparation for Henri's own death, when we held a wake and an all-night vigil and organized a three-hour funeral celebration.[6]

In my own life, both personally and professionally, I have discovered how profound this gift of presence can be. Both as a pastoral minister and a nurse, I have encountered times when, although I wanted to make someone "feel" better, there were no words to say. I am, by nature, a "nurturer," who always wants to fix things for people. However, in many situations, choosing to set aside the uneasiness of the moment to sit in silence with the person is the only option for a caring response.

One instance of this which stands out in my mind profoundly was a night when I was on duty in the emergency department, and we received a family of victims from a car accident. The mother was driving, and she was injured but not severely. The husband and daughter were killed, and the two young sons were critically injured and had to be airlifted to a larger trauma center.

The family was from out of town and their nearest relatives were hours away. They were virtually alone in our city. I was left caring for the obviously distraught mother, who kept rocking and crying, "I killed my family. Oh God, I killed my family!"

I had never felt so helpless in all my life. What could I say to comfort her? Her wounds were bandaged, but her soul was raw. I accompanied her to the morgue to say goodbye to her husband and daughter and held her as she wept. No words could bring comfort. My presence and my own tears were all I could offer her. As helpless as I felt, I knew it was the only way to care for her at that moment.

For people associated with hospice palliative care, the "presence" of caring has another nuance. Often, there is no further treatment available which will bring a cure for their illness. Hence, we sometimes hear this spoken of as being there "to care and not to cure."

> Care is something other than cure. Cure means "change." A doctor, a lawyer, a minister, a social worker—they all want to use their professional skills to bring about changes in people's lives. They get paid for whatever kind of cure they can bring about. But cure, desirable as it may be, can easily become violent, manipulative, and even destructive if it does not grow out of care. Care is being with, crying out with, suffering with, feeling with. Care is compassion. It is claiming the truth that the other person is my brother or sister, human, mortal, vulnerable, like I am.
>
> When care is our first concern, cure can be received as a gift. Often we are not able to cure, but we are always able to care. To care is to be human.[7]

Henri speaks in his writings about not only providing care for others, through presence, but also receiving care from others. Here Henri reflects on his hospital recuperation after the accident, when he was injured while going to care for Hsi-fu at one of the L'Arche homes.

One of the most life-giving experiences of my last weeks in the hospital was the visits of my father, my sister, friends and members of my community. They had time to spare. They had nothing more important to do. They could sit close to my bed and just be there. Especially the most handicapped were very present to me. Adam, Tracy, and Hsi-fu came in their wheelchairs. They didn't say anything, but they were there, just reminding me that I am loved as much as they are. . . . When Hsi-fu visited me, he jumped up and down in his wheelchair, and when I hugged him, he covered my face with his kisses. He made the circle full. I had wanted to come to him, but, in the end, it was he who came to me, as if to say: "Don't worry, I got my bath, but stay close to me so that you won't lose what you learned on your bed."[8]

Indeed, Henri reminds us that this mutuality of giving and receiving is the hallmark of living compassionately.

One of the most beautiful characteristics of the compassionate life is that there is always a mutuality of giving and receiving. Everyone who has truly entered into the compassionate life will say: "I have received as much as I have given." Those who have worked with the dying in Calcutta, . . . among the poor in the "young towns" of Lima . . . who have dedicated themselves to AIDS patients or mentally handicapped people—they all will express deep gratitude for the gifts received from those they came to help. There is probably no clearer sign of true compassion than this mutuality of giving and receiving.[9]

Developing trust and understanding through the gift of unhurried presence and becoming aware of the meaning of care are some of the ways to help build the relationships which enable those journeying with the dying to do it well. Often, the most difficult conversations of one's life take place during this time. The love and compassion expressed in these caring relationships will be the foundations for the safe place necessary in which to hold them.

THE GIFT OF TRUTH

Authors who work with the dying have written about this subject from different perspectives. Of course, Henri's is a spiritual background, and he has approached his interactions with those who are dying from that perspective. However, it is felt by many experts that being able to set aside one's fears to ask the hard questions and not to shy away from the answers is what is most desired by the caregivers as well as by the one who is facing death. Dr. David Kuhl, M.D., who has worked for years in palliative care in Vancouver, B.C., published an amazing book in 2002 titled *What Dying People Want*. In his introduction, he explains:

> Talking about dying is very difficult. We are afraid that talking about death beckons it. We all know death is inevitable; death fascinates and disturbs us; but we don't want it to happen. Maybe, we think, if we don't talk about death, death might not notice us. Maybe if we ignore death, we might delay or even elude it.
>
> For more than fifteen years I have worked, as a doctor, with people who were dying. They taught me many things—for example, that I didn't know how to talk to them about dying. And peculiar as it may seem, they taught me a lot about living.[10]

The book is the culmination of a ten-year study, a collection of stories of people who knew that they were dying. He interviewed them, wanting to hear about their experiences of living with a terminal illness, especially with regards to the psychological and spiritual issues they were facing at the end of their life.

> [T]oo many people wait too long to begin the inward journey of learning who they are, what the meaning of life might be for them, the value of relationships and of spirituality.
>
> Time is now. That was one of the major lessons I learned in spending time with people who knew they were dying. Time pass-

es quickly. People wait for the optimal circumstances for intimate conversations. They wait for the courage to do what they have never done before. But then the illness progresses faster than anticipated. (Doctors predict three to twelve months of life remaining, but people only hear that they have twelve months.) Fatigue sets in. (I'll do this tomorrow; I might have more energy then.) Cancer affects thought processes (body chemistry, side effects of medication, metastases to the brain, low oxygen supply). People who may not have a specific diagnosis of a terminal illness but are aging wait for the doctor to inform them that they are dying before they take time seriously. They think difficult conversations can happen later. But will they? And will they be any easier once the terminal illness has been diagnosed? Will they be easier at age eighty-five than they are at age fifty-eight?[11]

In another wonderful book, *Final Gifts*, Maggie Callanan and Patricia Kelley tell us stories about communication with those who are dying and the importance of talking about death.

It's common, initially, for the family to greet the hospice nurse with a warning: "Don't say anything to her about dying. She doesn't know and she couldn't handle it!" Moments later, the patient tells the nurse privately: "Don't say anything to my family about my dying. They don't know and they couldn't handle it!" With support and encouragement both patient and family can end this compassionate conspiracy and move on to honest, open communication.[12]

We hear the same message about speaking the truth from one of the beloved experts on dying, Morrie Schwartz. Morrie, who died of ALS (Lou Gehrig's disease) in 1995, was the inspiring hero of *Tuesdays with Morrie*, written by Mitch Albom, who spent Tuesdays interviewing his old teacher and friend, and writing down the reflections he had about living and dying—and a host of other things! Morrie tells us to "Talk openly about your illness

with those who'll listen. It will help them cope with their own vul-
nerabilities as well as your own."[13]

Henri's friends have all said how open and honest he was, and
how that changed the way many of them viewed their own
responses to life's struggles. Of course, Henri believed that Jesus,
by the way he lived and died, was the one who really showed us
how to live in truth and not to be afraid.

> Jesus' attitude was quite different. He encountered suffering and
> death with his eyes wide open. Actually, his whole life was a con-
> scious preparation for them. Jesus doesn't commend them as desir-
> able things; but he does speak of them as realities we ought not to
> repudiate, avoid, or cover up.
>
> On a number of occasions he foretold his own suffering and
> death. . . . [H]e tells his disciples . . . very plainly, that a person who
> wants to lead a spiritual life cannot do so without the prospect of
> suffering and death. . . . "If anyone wants to be a follower of mine,
> let him renounce himself and take up his cross and follow me.
> Anyone who wants to save his life will lose it; but anyone who loses
> his life for my sake will find it."
>
> Finding new life through suffering and death: that is the core
> of the good news. Jesus has lived out that liberating way before us
> and made it the great sign.[14]

Wendy Lywood, an Anglican priest who lives at L'Arche
Daybreak, talks about how working with Henri while he was pastor there deeply influenced her ministry. Moving to Daybreak
came at a time in Wendy's life when she was frustrated by the fact
that her vision of Christian community and the reality of her life
in the parish didn't match anymore.

> For example, I really believed the church has an important min-
> istry in being with people in the experience of dying and death,
> but I was frustrated by my inability to break through the cultural

taboos about death. I was longing to find a genuine Christian response to the reality of death, but I knew that unless I could talk honestly about death I couldn't talk about the resurrection in an authentic way.[15]

Working with Henri not only opened her up to new ways of talking about death, but also new ways of looking at her ministry, as well as herself. He reminded her, "Wendy, remember the ministry is about being present with people as you are, not as you are not. You won't say anything new or original, just speak from your heart and from your own relationship with Jesus. You're not there to solve problems but to announce that Jesus wants to love, heal, forgive, and reconcile."[16]

In an interview I had with her, she shared with me how, although "Henri could be flighty, he could also be right there in the moment. He was a gifted pastor with a gifted, pastoral presence. He was open, and not afraid to say what he was thinking. It was refreshing for me. His lack of fear brought freedom to a situation. He also had the ability to bring the Word of God to any situation."[17]

One profound example of how Henri was not afraid to talk about dying was Wendy's recollection of an encounter he had with his secretary, Connie Ellis, who was dying of a brain tumor. On a visit to the hospital that she made with Henri, Wendy tells us what transpired:

I waited near the back of the room as Henri and Connie greeted one another. The image I have is of Henri's large frame bent over and enveloping Connie, as if he were a bird protecting its young. He took her hand tenderly in his; then he asked me if I would read the Gospel for the day. It was from Luke 4, where Jesus reads from the scroll of the prophet Isaiah. Henri then spoke with gentle authority: "Connie, this reading has a special meaning for you. You are poor as you face your death, but Jesus wants you to know that he has

good news for you: that he will not abandon you even as you journey through death. You are captive now in your body, but you will
be released. You are blind now, because you can't see what lies
ahead, but you will soon see anew in the kingdom of God. You are
oppressed now, but soon you will be free." I was shocked at first by
Henri's directness, but there was also a great longing awakened
within me; a truth was being spoken that I needed to hear.

Henri taught me and our community a lot about how to
befriend death. We walked through it with Maurice, Connie, Hank,
Lloyd, Helen, and Adam. Each time we learned to trust more that
when we could share our deepest sorrows, we would touch in the
same place our deepest joys. Henri helped us articulate that joy and
sorrow are two sides of the same coin.[18]

Ridding ourselves of our fears to talk about death was something Henri wrote about openly. His honesty in facing the truth
was also captured in print by others. Joseph Cardinal Bernardin,
the Archbishop of Chicago until his death from pancreatic cancer
in 1996, writes about Henri in his book *The Gift of Peace.*

A very significant thing happened during the month of July last
year. Father Henri Nouwen, a friend of mine for more than twenty-
five years, paid me a visit. He had come to a conference in the met-
ropolitan area and asked if he could come to see me. I said, "By all
means." We spent over an hour together, and he brought me one
of his latest books, *Our Greatest Gift: A Reflection on Dying and
Caring.* We talked about the book, and the main thing I remember
is that he talked about the importance of looking on death as a
friend rather than an enemy. While I had always taken such a view
in terms of my faith, I needed to be reminded at that moment
because I was rather exhausted from the radiation treatments. "It's
very simple," he said. "If you have fear and anxiety and you talk to
a friend, then those fears and anxieties are minimized and could
even disappear. If you see them as an enemy, then you go into a

state of denial and try to get as far away as possible from them."
He said, "People of faith, who believe that death is the transition
from this life to life eternal, should see it as a friend."

   This conversation was a great help to me. It removed some of
my anxiety or fear about death for myself. When Father Nouwen
died suddenly of a heart attack on September 21 of this year at the
age of 64, everyone was shocked. Yet, there is no doubt that he
was prepared. He spent a lifetime teaching others how to live, and
how to die.[19]

Once the truth is spoken, and the conversation has begun,
there are many things that can be done or talked about which will
help someone live their dying. Perhaps it will be helpful for you
to encourage them to review their life. This might be done
through informal sharing of memories, or in a more formal way of
preparing a life review or life story book. Jane Powell, who has
worked with the L'Arche community for many years, explains this
idea for us.

   The preparation of a life story book can be a therapeutic project
   during the time of anticipatory grief. It can also be a very good way
   for a terminally ill person to integrate his or her life experiences and
   the book itself can be a wonderful legacy for friends and relatives.
   The therapeutic effect may actually be experienced both by the
   helper and by the one being helped, as together they examine the
   many ups and downs of the subject's life journey and the experiences that have shaped who the person has become. And the book
   itself can be a wonderful legacy for the deceased person to leave
   behind for family and friends.[20]

Callanan and Kelley also talk about this practice.

   [A] mental inventory of accomplishments and disappointments . . .
   can be done orally, in the company of family and friends; or in writ-

ing, as a life history to be passed on to the next generation; or as letters to young children to be read when they're older.

Most dying people begin by listing their accomplishments, but they also will consider disappointments—tasks not completed, opportunities missed, relationships broken or left to wither. As caregivers or friends, if we can help dying people conduct such reviews and heal damaged relationships, we can help them find peace.

Most people, as they're dying, want to feel that their having been alive has been significant, that they made some difference in this world and in the lives of those around them. For all of us, some periodic review of how our lives are going, and recognition of our achievements, may help us find more enjoyment and purpose in our lives. At the same time some recognition of our "unfinished business" or troubled relationships may lead us to try to heal some problem areas now, rather than waiting until we are dying. This could enrich our lives and prevent frantic attempts at reconciliation when it is almost too late.[21]

In Chapter 4, we heard Henri talk about the need for forgiveness and reconciliation in order to make the first step from mourning to dancing. Those who journey with the dying may be able to assist them to see the need for this and help them to carry it out. Henri speaks again of this truth, and also of the model we have for this difficult task, in the person of Jesus.

What makes us cling to life even when it is time to "move on"? Is it our unfinished business? Sometimes we cling to life because we have not yet been able to say, "I forgive you, and I ask for your forgiveness." When we have forgiven those who have hurt us and asked forgiveness from those we have hurt, a new freedom emerges. It is the freedom to move on.

When Jesus was dying he prayed for those who had nailed him to the cross: "Father, forgive them; they do not know what they are doing" (Luke 23:34). That prayer set him free to say, "Father, into your hands I commit my spirit" (Luke 23:46).[22]

Another task that may need to be filled by the caregiver and/or family is to give the dying the permission to die. Often, it seems as though people hang on and don't want to leave their loved ones behind. They may be afraid that their loved ones are not ready for them to go, even though they themselves may be ready.

> One of the greatest gifts we can offer our family and friends is helping them to die well. Sometimes they are ready to go to God but we have a hard time letting them go. But there is a moment in which we need to give those we love the permission to return to God, from whom they came. We have to sit quietly with them and say, "Do not be afraid. . . . I love you, God loves you. . . . It's time for you to go in peace. . . . I won't cling to you any longer. . . . I set you free to go home. . . . Go gently, go with my love." Saying this from the heart is a true gift. It is the greatest gift love can give.
>
> When Jesus died he said, "Father, into your hands I commit my Spirit" (Luke 23:46). It is good to repeat these words often to our dying friends. With these words on their lips or in their hearts, they can make the passage as Jesus did.[23]

It is such an honor and a privilege to journey with someone through their life and death. Those are sacred moments, where God is indeed present.

THE MINISTRY OF HEALING

Henri has written in many of his books about compassion, ministry, and healing. He tells us that the definition of "compassion" is similar to the definition of "care." "The word 'compassion' is derived from the Latin words *pati* and *cum*, which together mean 'to suffer with.' Compassion asks us to go where it hurts, to enter into places of pain, to share in brokenness, fear, confusion, and anguish. . . . Compassion means full immersion in the condition of being human."[24]

> If there is one notion that is central to all great religions it is that of "compassion." The sacred scriptures of the Hindus, Buddhists, Moslems, Jews, and Christians all speak about God as the God of compassion. In a world in which competition continues to be the dominant mode of relating among people, be it in politics, sports, or economics, all true believers proclaim compassion, not competition, as God's way. . . .
>
> Still, Jesus says: "Be compassionate as your heavenly Father is compassionate," and throughout the centuries all great spiritual guides echo these words. Compassion—which means, literally, "to suffer with"—is the way to the truth that we are most ourselves, not when we differ from others, but when we are the same. Indeed, the main spiritual question is not, "What difference do you make?" but "What do you have in common?" It is not "excelling" but "serving" that makes us most human. It is not proving ourselves to be better than others but confessing to be just like others that is the way to healing and reconciliation.
>
> Compassion, to be with others when and where they suffer and to willingly enter into a fellowship of the weak, is God's way to justice and peace among people. Is this possible? Yes, it is, but only when we dare to live with the radical faith that we do not have to compete for love, but that love is freely given to us by the One who calls us to compassion.[25]

However, Nouwen also tells us that:

> Compassion is not a skill that we can master by arduous training, years of study, or careful supervision. We cannot get a Master's degree or a Ph.D. in compassion. Compassion is a divine gift and

not a result of systematic study or effort . . . compassion is not conquered but given, not the outcome of our hard work but the fruit of God's grace.[26]

If this is true, then every one of us can be called upon to be compassionate, to be instruments of God's healing and grace in the lives of others. When we have not had any special training, we might wonder if we can make a difference in the life of someone who is suffering or dying. We might feel inadequate or unsure of ourselves. And yet, this is exactly when God can work tremendous miracles of peace and grace through us. If we do not see ourselves as experts, and realize that we rely on God to give us wisdom and strength and direction in what to say or how to care for someone, that is precisely when God will use our hands and our hearts as an expression of divine love. That is when God can choose to love someone through us. So often we don't have confidence in ourselves and believe that only "professionals" can be ministers or healers.

It is important to realize that you cannot get a Ph.D. in caring, that caring cannot be delegated to specialists, and that therefore nobody can be excused from caring. Still, in a society like ours, we have a strong tendency to refer to specialists. When someone does not feel well, we quickly think, "Where can we find a doctor?" When someone is confused, we easily advise him to go to a counselor. And when someone is dying, we quickly call a priest. Even when someone wants to pray we wonder if there is a minister around. . . .

Although it is usually very meaningful to call on outside help, sometimes our referral to others is more a sign of fear to face the pain than a sign of care, and in that case we keep our greatest gift to heal hidden from each other. Every human being has a great, yet often unknown, gift to care, to be compassionate, to become present to the other, to listen, to hear and to receive. If that gift would be set free and made available, miracles could take place. . . . Those who can sit in silence with their fellow man, not knowing what to say, but knowing that they should be there, can bring new life in a dying heart.[27]

Nouwen believed that all of us could be called to be ministers and healers.

Ministry is entering with our human brokenness into communion with others and speaking a word of hope. This hope is not based on any power to solve the problems of those with whom we live, but on the love of God, which becomes visible when we let go of our fears of being out of control and enter into his presence in a shared confession of weakness.

This is a hard vocation. It goes against the grain of our need for self-affirmation, self-fulfillment, and self-realization. It is a call to true humility.[28]

The great vocation of the minister is to continuously make connections between the human story and the divine story. We have inherited a story which needs to be told in such a way that the many painful wounds about which we hear day after day can be liberated from their isolation and be revealed as part of God's relationship with us. Healing means revealing that our human wounds are most intimately connected with the suffering of God himself.[29]

It is this element of faith and belief in the life, death, and resurrection of Jesus, the Christ, which denotes the distinction between activism and Christian action. As we know, there are many people who are caring and compassionate but who do not profess to be Christian, nor do they connect themselves with God. However, those who live a spiritual life and "have entered deeply into their hearts and found the intimate home where they encounter their Lord . . . come to the awareness that the intimacy of God's house excludes no one and includes everyone. They start to see that the home they have found in their innermost being is as wide as the whole of humanity."[30]

All Christian action—whether it is visiting the sick, feeding the hungry, clothing the naked, or working for a more just and peaceful society—is a manifestation of the human solidarity revealed to us in the house of God. It is not an anxious human effort to create a better world. It is a confident expression of the truth that in Christ, death, evil, and destruction have been overcome. It is not a fearful attempt to restore a broken order. It is a joyful assertion that in Christ all order has already been restored. It is not a nervous effort to bring divided people together, but a celebration of an already established unity. Thus action is not activism. An activist wants to heal, restore, redeem, and re-create, but those acting within the house of God point through their action to the healing, restoring, redeeming, and re-creating presence of God.[31]

Those who care with eyes of faith, believing their ministry, compassion, and healing flow through them from a God of infinite love, will find it necessary to spend time alone with God. It is during these moments that they will develop an intimate relationship with the One who is their source of wisdom, strength, compassion, peace, and unconditional love.

SUSTAINING THE CAREGIVER

We talked in earlier chapters about the importance of prayer in reminding us of our identity as God's beloved. Solitude, letting ourselves sit quietly in God's presence, is essential. "Prayer means entering into communion with the One who loved us before we could love. It is this 'first love' (1 Jn 4:19) that is revealed to us in prayer. . . . In the house of God we were created. To that house we are called to return. Prayer is the act of returning."[32] Prayer is the discipline of listening to the voice of God, the inner voice of love. Henri reminds us:

> To live a Christian life means to live in the world without being of it. It is in solitude that this inner freedom can grow. Jesus went to a lonely place to pray, that is, to grow in the awareness that all the power he had was given to him; that all the words he spoke came from his Father; and that all the works he did were not really his, but the works of the One who had sent him.[33]

"If we heal by reminding each other of God in Christ, then we must have the mind of Christ himself to do so. For that, prayer is indispensable."[34] So how does one set one's heart on the kingdom and begin to develop the mind of Christ?

> Whatever concrete method we use to set our minds and hearts on the kingdom, it is important only in that it brings us closer to our Lord. The attentive repetition of a prayer is one method that has proven to be fruitful. Another is the contemplation of the daily Gospel. Each day of the year has its own Gospel passage. Each passage holds its own treasure for us. For me it has been of immense spiritual value to read each morning the story about Jesus that has been chosen for the day and to look at it and listen to it with my inner eyes and ears. I have discovered that when I do this over a long period of time, the life of Jesus becomes more and more alive in me and starts to guide me in my daily activities.
>
> Often I have found myself saying: "The Gospel that I read this morning was just what I needed today!" This was much more than a wonderful coincidence. What, in fact, was taking place was not that a Gospel text helped me with a concrete problem, but that the many Gospel passages that I had been contemplating were gradually giving me new eyes and new ears to see and hear what was happening in the world. It wasn't that the Gospel proved useful for

my many worries but that the Gospel proved the uselessness of my worries and so refocused my whole attention.[35]

And so, we are reminded of what it is that will truly sustain the minister, the healer, the caregiver.

[T]o be a healing reminder requires a spirituality, a spiritual connectedness, a way of living united with God. What does this imply for the daily life of the minister?

It implies that prayer, not in the sense of *prayers,* but in the sense of a prayerful life, a life lived in connection with Christ, should be our first and overriding concern.

It implies that in a life of connectedness with Christ the needs of our neighbors and the nature of our service are disclosed.

It implies that all training and formation are intended to facilitate this disclosure, and that the insights of the behavioral sciences should be seen as aids in this process.

It implies that prayer cannot be considered external to the process of ministry.[36]

Finally, listen to your heart. It's there that Jesus speaks most intimately to you. Praying is first and foremost listening to Jesus, who dwells in the very depths of your heart. He doesn't shout. He doesn't thrust himself upon you. His voice is an unassuming voice, very nearly a whisper, the voice of a gentle love. . . . This listening must be an active and very attentive listening, for in our restless and noisy world Jesus' loving voice is easily drowned out. You need to set aside some time every day for this active listening to Jesus, if only for ten minutes. Ten minutes each day for Jesus alone can bring about a radical change in your life.[37]

"When you come to see Jesus more and more as the compassionate God, you will begin increasingly to see your own life as one in which you yourself want to express that divine compassion. . . . [Y]ou feel a deep longing within you to make your own life a life for others. Living for other people in solidarity with the compassionate Jesus: that's what it means to live a spiritual life."[38]

When we live a spiritual life, a life truly lived for others, we will find tremendous peace in our hearts. Spending time in prayer will also foster this peace in our hearts, even if there is little peace around us. Etty Hillesum, a Jewish woman who was a prisoner during World War II, explains this concept in her own eloquent way:

> Ultimately, we have just one moral duty:
> to reclaim large areas of peace in ourselves,
> more and more peace
> and to reflect it towards others.
> And the more peace there is in us,
> the more peace there will also be in our troubled world.[39]

Sometimes it is hard for us, even though we take time to pray, to make the connections with the suffering Christ and those whom we care for and minister to. However, it is only through prayerful reflection that God will reveal that to us. Henri was someone who, although he struggled with his prayer life and wrote freely about those struggles, nonetheless, persevered. He spent time each day alone with God, time celebrating Eucharist with others, and was ultimately given the gift of being able to express these reflections in a form that has been made available to us through his writings. His writings, the fruit of his reflections on the presence of God in his life, help us to be able to do the same. "My hope is that the description of God's love in my life will give you the freedom and the courage to discover—and maybe also describe—God's love in yours."[40]

Henri writes about how Christ has been present to him through his friend Adam, after living through the days in and around Adam's death and funeral liturgy. Perhaps it will help in your own reflections on when Christ has been present to you.

As I have lived these last three days, I've come to see with a clarity I never had before that Adam was the living Christ among us. Where else did we have to go to be with the man of sorrow and the man of joy? Where else did we have to look for the presence of God? Yes, Adam was loved by God long before his parents, his brother, or we, loved him. Yes, Adam was sent by God to live among us, a hard but blessed life for thirty-four years. And yes, Adam, after completing his mission, was called back home to God to live a new life in a new body. That's the story of Jesus. That's the story of Adam too![41]

Another gift that certainly sustains the caregiver is the peace and joy that comes from living the compassionate life. Although the world tells us that joy comes from success, power, and popularity, we have seen that these can also leave us quite unfulfilled and even depressed. Henri talks about the kind of joy which sustained him as he cared for Adam.

The joy that compassion brings is one of the best-kept secrets of humanity. It is a secret known to only a very few people, a secret that has to be rediscovered over and over again.

I have had a few glimpses of it. When I came to Daybreak, a community with people who have mental disabilities, I was asked to spend a few hours with Adam, one of the handicapped members of the community. Each morning I had to get him out of bed, give him a bath, shave him, brush his teeth, comb his hair, dress him, walk him to the kitchen, give him his breakfast, and bring him to the place where he spends his day. During the first few weeks, I was mostly afraid, always worrying that I would do something wrong or that he would have an epileptic seizure. But gradually I relaxed and started to enjoy our daily routine. As the weeks passed by, I discovered how I had come to look forward to my two hours with Adam. Whenever I thought of him during the day, I experienced gratitude for having him as my friend. Even though he couldn't speak or even give a sign of recognition, there was real love between us. My time with Adam had become the most precious time of the day. When a visiting friend asked me one day: "Couldn't you spend your time better than working with this handicapped man? Was it for this type of work that you got all your education?" I realized that I couldn't explain to him the joy that Adam brought me. He had to discover that for himself.

Joy is the secret gift of compassion. We keep forgetting it and thoughtlessly look elsewhere. But each time we return to where there is pain, we get a new glimpse of the joy that is not of this world.[42]

Although there is much joy to be found in our compassionate encounters with others, we also know how difficult it can be and how tired we become, especially when we give to others intensely, or over long periods of time.

When we are asked to listen to the pains of people and empathize with their suffering, we soon reach our emotional limits. We can only listen for a short time and only to a few people. In our society we are bombarded with so much "news" about human misery that our hearts easily get numbed simply because of overload.

But God's compassionate heart does not have limits. God's heart is greater, infinitely greater, than the human heart. It is that divine heart that God wants to give to us so that we can love all people without burning out or becoming numb.[43]

In an interview in 1996 for the University of Notre Dame, Henri shares some insights about how to avoid caregiver burnout.

- Burnout is giving without receiving. The caregiver always needs to review this perspective and support one another and see the gifts of the ones we care for. It is a spiritual challenge to discover the gifts of the aging and dying, and realize they prepare us for something. God said, "Blessed are the poor" (the old, the dying, the dependent, the handicapped), not, "Blessed are those who care for them." It is important for the caregiver to truly believe and perceive that God's blessing is rooted in the poverty of those for whom I care and that I can only be a caregiver if I can receive even more than I give.

- To be a good caregiver is to be really present—as in the ministry of presence.
- It is important not to be alone as a caregiver, and to be aware of limits.
- Caregivers have to realize when it's necessary for them to have a time-out and not to feel guilty about it.
- It is important to be cared for yourself, as a caregiver. Who holds you? This is necessary so that you can be totally there when you are caregiving, and trust that when you leave your presence will continue.
- One of the most difficult things is to be only half there—to be present but not want to be. This leads to resentment.[44]

It is vitally important for the caregiver to realize that he or she is not alone. They must not only stay connected to the community that gives them their own strength but also not be afraid to ask for the spiritual, emotional, and, many times, physical help of this community to assist in giving strength to the one who is dying, and to their family and friends. It is only as a community, the "Body of Christ," that we can serve as Christ did. "No one person can fulfill all your needs. But the community can truly hold you. The community can let you experience the fact that, beyond your anguish, there are human hands that hold you and show you God's faithful love."[45]

CARING AS A COMMUNITY

It is easy for generous Christians to find themselves losing their spirit and feeling more and more tired, not because the work is too hard or they don't feel successful, but because they are feeling isolated, unsupported, and virtually alone. People may begin to wonder if anyone really cares what they are doing out there or if the people from the community who sent them out ever think about them or pray for them. It is easy to lose faith when we no longer experience ourselves as a part of a loving, caring, supportive community. "Without a sense of being sent by a caring community, a compassionate life cannot last long and quickly degenerates into a life marked by numbness and anger. This is not simply a psychological observation, but a theological truth, because apart from a vital relationship with a caring community a vital relationship with Christ is not possible." [46]

To care for others as they become weaker and closer to death is to allow them to fulfill their deepest vocation, that of becoming evermore fully what they already are: daughters and sons of God. It is to help them to claim, especially in their dying hours, their divine childhood and to let the Spirit of God cry out from their hearts, "Abba, Father" (Galatians 4:9). To care for the dying is to keep saying, "You are the beloved daughter of God, you are the beloved son of God."

How do we say this? The ways are countless: through words, prayers, and blessings; through gentle touch and the holding of hands; through cleaning and feeding; through listening and just being there. . . .Through our caring presence, we keep announcing that sacred truth: dying is not a sweet, sentimental event; it is a great struggle to surrender our lives completely.

. . . I don't believe we can care in this way on our own. . . . Reminding people in their agony of their divine childhood is not something we can do on our own. The powers of darkness are strong, and we can easily be pulled into the darkness ourselves and drawn into enormous self-doubts. To stand by a person who is dying is to participate in the immense struggle of faith. It is a struggle no person should take on alone. . . .

No, we shouldn't try to care by ourselves. Care is not an endurance test. We should, whenever possible, care together with others. It is the community of care that reminds the dying person of his or her belovedness. . . . Together, as a body of love, as a community that cares, we can come close to the dying and discover there a new hope, a new life, and a new strength to live. There can be smiles and stories, new encounters and new knowledge about ways to help, beautiful moments of silence and prayer. There can be the gift of people being together, waiting patiently for death to come. Together we can create that place where our dying friends can feel safe and can gradually let go and make the passage knowing that they are loved.[47]

Henri wrote these reflections about the caring community in his book *Our Greatest Gift.* However, he wrote not from theory, but from lived experience. He learned about living in community and caring as a community in his day-to-day encounters with Adam and with others at L'Arche. He learned this also from his journeying with family and friends through their dying.

Adam's total dependence made it possible for him to live fully only if we lived in a loving community around him. His great teaching to us was, "I can live only if you surround me with love and if you love one another. Otherwise, my life is useless and I am a burden." Adam truly challenged us to trust that compassion, not competition, is the way to fulfill our human vocation.[48]

Henri also shared some reflections of a conversation he had with his secretary, Connie, as she battled brain cancer. Connie was preparing herself for her own death, and was confiding in Henri about her feelings for her grandchildren, Charles and Sarah. "I don't want the kids to suffer because of me. I don't want them to become sad and sorrowful as they see me dying. They always knew me as the strong grandmother they could count on.

They don't know me as a paralyzed woman whose hair is falling out because of radiation therapy."[49] Henri wrote that he could see how Connie, most of all, wanted everyone to be happy. She seemed to care more deeply about their well-being than her own. Yet, he wanted her to see that having them involved in her dying would, in itself, be fruitful.

> I wanted her to come to see that, in her growing dependence, she is giving more to her grandchildren than during the times when she could bring them in her car to school, to shops, and to sports fields. I wanted her to discover that the times when she needs them are as important as the times when they need her. In fact, in her illness, she has become their real teacher. She speaks to them about her gratitude for life, her trust in God, and her hope in a life beyond death. She shows them real thankfulness for all the little things they do for her. She doesn't keep her tears or fears hidden when they suddenly well up, but she always returns to a smile.
>
> . . . Now, in her growing weakness, she who lived such a long and productive life gives what she couldn't give in her strength: a glimpse of the truth that love is stronger than death. Her grandchildren will reap the full fruits of that truth.[50]

In *Befriending Life*, Connie's daughter-in-law, Carmen, adds this reflection about the effect Connie's dying did have on Charles and Sarah, and the fact that Henri foresaw the fruits of her dying for them.

> And this was true. This is what happened. We were blessed in supporting her those two years. Our children, Sarah and Charles, helped her a lot. Not that it wasn't hard. But she was always so thankful. And before, Mom didn't really speak about her relationship with God, but now she mentioned her faith often. She was amazing.[51]

Harold Ivan Smith has written a wonderful book titled
*Finding Your Way to Say Goodbye: Comfort for the Dying and Those Who
Care for Them.* In his opening pages he encourages those who are
facing death not to shut people out. He knows the value of the
community that will surround the one who is entering this final
stage of life. As Henri encouraged Connie to include her grandchildren in her care and to allow them to support her as she
became more dependent, so Harold encourages his readers to do
the same.

It will not be wise for you to put up a "Do NOT disturb!" sign.
You need others. This is a drama, not a one actor show.
        Ignore the temptation to be The Loner.
You will not be doing friends a favor
        by keeping them from walking with you
        on this portion of the shadowed trail.
This is not time for bravado or tough "I can take its!"
        Or to dust off your best imitation of tough guys
        John Wayne, Charles Bronson, or Sylvester Stallone.
If you make the choice to pretend "tough,"
        you exclude loved ones and friends
        and all those who made up the "others" of your life
        from walking beside you on a path, that sooner or later,
        they too must walk.
If you exclude individuals, you keep them
        from witnessing your dying
        and learning from your dying
        and growing from your dying.
You keep them from the lessons that cannot be found
        in a book or homily or lecture or video.
Indeed, some of the knowledge you will need you might have
                known
        if only someone had let you in on her dying.[52]

Surrounding ourselves with our family and friends, being able to live until we die and enjoy each moment, will bring fruits of joy—not only to the dying person but to those who care for them. Smith describes this further on at the beginning of his book.

> A WOMAN, now dying, loved chocolate milkshakes.
> At 2:00 a.m., a heartbroken friend
> wiping away tears, drove until she found an all night diner
> and bought a dozen milkshakes. Chocolate, of course.
> In the middle of that last night
> family, friends, nurses, chaplain gathered for one final
> toast
> and sipped milkshakes as Judy tasted her last sip
> then breathed her last.
> It was a "Judy" moment. A gift for the memories.
> They "made love." Real love.
> And, in a way, they all received provision for their journey
> into a land without Judy.
> People still talk about milkshakes at 2:00 a.m.!
> Or was it Eucharist at 2:00 a.m.?
> YOU have to find YOUR way in this dying.
> But you do not have to figure it out by yourself.
> And sometimes, you have to put down the map,
> and take a long look out the windshield and say,
> "I think it's this way." [53]

Only by claiming our gift of care and embracing other people's mortality as well as our own, can we become true sources of healing and hope. It means letting go of our need to cure, and having the courage to care, with the compassion of the One who loved us first. This allows us to heal in ways that far exceed our own dreams and expectations. It also gives us the gifts we will need to embrace the next step of grieving.

CARE FOR THE GRIEVING

One thing is for sure—wherever there is dying, no matter how well it is experienced, there will be grief. There is grief not only for the person dying, as they look at all of their gradual losses, including the loss of their very life, but also for all those who have journeyed with them. Grief, in some form or another, will encompass their loved ones, family, friends, faith community, workplace community, the medical community of caregivers, and an endless circle of people who have been touched deeply by knowing them. Grieving can be a painful journey, but like dying, it can also be a fruitful journey.

> When we lose a dear friend, someone we have loved deeply, we are left with a grief that can paralyze us emotionally for a long time. People we love become part of us. Our thinking, feeling, and acting are codetermined by them: Our fathers, our mothers, our husbands, our wives, our lovers, our children, our friends—they all are living in our hearts. When they die a part of us dies too. That is what grief is about: It is that slow and painful departure of someone who has become an intimate part of us. When Christmas, the new year, a birthday, or an anniversary comes, we feel deeply the absence of our beloved companion. We sometimes have to live a whole year or more before our hearts have fully said good-bye and the pain of our grief recedes. But as we let go of them they become part of our "members," and as we "re-member" them they become guides on our spiritual journey.[54]

Henri grieved deeply the loss of his mother, with whom he was very close. In a prayer he wrote while staying at the Genesee Abbey, he recalled how his own grief in not being able to see her again was comforted with Scripture, and also with the knowledge that her life would continue to bear fruit.

O Lord, your abundant love became visible today in the abundant beauty of nature. The sun covered the wide fields of the Genesee Valley. . . . I looked from the ridge out over the valley and was overwhelmed by the stark beauty of the world in which I am living. I was filled with a sense of gratitude, but also with a sense of the shortness of life. When I saw the rich soil, I thought of mother being buried in similar soil only a few months ago, and a strange sadness welled up within the experience of beauty. I can no longer tell her about what I saw, nor can I write her about the new spring, which she always welcomed with much joy. New life, new green leaves, new flowers, new wheat; but this spring she would not call my name and say, "Look here, look there!"

But you, O Lord, say, "The grain of wheat must die to yield a rich harvest." I believe that her death will yield fruits. The day of your resurrection for which I am preparing myself is also a sign that there is hope for all who die. So, let my sadness be a sorrow that makes me more eager to follow you on the way to the cross and beyond it, to that Easter morning with its empty grave.

Let the beauty of the land deepen my joy as well as my sorrow, and thus draw me closer to you, my Lord and my Redeemer. Amen.[55]

Henri can guide us again in how to walk the journey of grief, not only with his writings, but also through his example. Many stories abound about how Henri grieved publicly and, by doing so, gave others the courage to do so too. By not being afraid to face the truth with others about his feelings, he seemed to give them permission to express their own emotions. This was particularly true with the differently-abled people with whom he lived at L'Arche. Wendy Lywood shared some moments which help describe how Henri walked with his community through grief.

I remember that after Lloyd Kerman died we gathered in the chapel. Henri was sitting at the front and asking people to share what Lloyd's death meant to them. Michael Arnett, one of Lloyd's good friends, cried out, "My heart is broken! What does it mean, my heart is broken?" Michael's question pierced through our grief. Henri leapt out of his chair and ran to kneel in front of Michael. "It means you have a heart that loves and that you especially loved Lloyd, Michael. Now that Lloyd has died, your heart has a big hole in it; that is why it hurts so much." I was moved not only by Michael's honesty and ability to articulate his pain but also by Henri's response. It was not so much what he said but the way his whole being became compassion. It seemed to me that both Michael and Henri were both profoundly incarnational—Michael's pain and Henri's compassion were both experienced in the fullness of their humanity. In the Gospels when we are told that Jesus had compassion for the people, the Greek word used means that he was moved in his guts. Henri was following in the footsteps of Jesus in being such a compassionate pastor—he didn't hold back in fear, he didn't need to keep a professional distance.[56]

Jane Powell tells us, from her experience with the differently-abled, that there are different steps we can take to help others grieve. I believe these steps are the same for all of us. They include:

- Sharing the news fully and clearly at the time of death.
- Gathering together soon after a death.
- Helping those who are grieving to be involved in the rituals.
- Being present with one another.
- Visiting the grave and celebrating anniversaries.
- Giving permission to grieve.
- Naming the gifts and also the difficult realities of the person who has died.

In reflecting on her own experience of being present with someone during a difficult time, she recalls:

Almost all people wish to have another person whom they trust simply be present with them at a time of intense grief. When Henri died suddenly of a heart attack it was difficult for all of us at Daybreak. He had helped many of us in the community when other members had died, so that we especially missed his comfort when he himself passed away. I had the privilege of sitting at his wake with Tracy, a woman who needs much support because she has profound cerebral palsy. We sat together in silence on some cushions on the floor near the coffin containing Henri's body, with Tracy leaning against me. We had no words to share that would comfort us because Tracy does not speak with words and because my words would not have made our grief any easier. But being there quietly with Tracy was very consoling for me. We needed to be together. It was one of those privileged moments when our common humanity is evident and differences fade away.[57]

Wendy Lywood also reflects on how Henri himself had a passion about wakes. Again, what is true for the needs of the core members is usually true for the needs of all of us, although we are often not as open about identifying what is helpful for us, or accepting that help.

Henri . . . and other leaders in the community knew that for the core members to grieve well they needed to participate in concrete ways in the mourning process. Henri encouraged people to come to the open casket, to touch the body, to leave a drawing or memento, and to pray. . . . Henri greeted us all and invited us to listen to Scripture. He then asked a few people who had been close to the person who died to share stories about their relationship.

The deep quality of the sharing had a lot to do with the core members' ability to express their feelings, but Henri's ministry allowed their natural gifts to blossom and bless everyone there. This was a far cry from the hushed tones and awkwardness of my previous visits to a funeral home. The result was a deeply healing experience of community as we cried our sorrows and laughed our love. It was so hopeful. I began to discover that it is the journey into the reality of death that allows us to find hope springing from our shared grief. It sounds obvious, but the only way to get to the hope offered in the resurrection is to go through death, not around it.[58]

Talking about death and those who had died, and celebrating their lives with stories and picnics and storybooks, was something for which Henri will always be remembered. Because he struggled openly with his own insecurities and pain, he seemed to be intuitive when it came to recognizing someone else's fear or pain, even when they couldn't see it themselves. He spent his time trying to help others let go of their fears, and to find ways to express the love they had for their deceased relatives and friends more openly.

Sally Tucker, a friend of the L'Arche Daybreak community, experienced Henri's openness and encouragement when she was struggling to find a way to celebrate the fifth anniversary of her husband Bob's death. Her children were very young when he died, and they found it difficult to go with her to visit his grave. She asked Henri if he would help them find a new way to visit the grave, and he enthusiastically said, "Yes!" On arriving at the cemetery, Henri asked nine-year-old Mitchell, who was only four when his dad died, to tell him stories about what he could remember. Henri also shared stories about his growing up, and together they planted a flower that Henri had brought, as they sat on the grass at the grave.

We laughed as he shared more stories about himself growing up. I remember Henri's gentleness with Mitchell. The time was easy for the three of us, and I knew I had found what I was so longing for— a new way of being with Bob for me and my children.

Henri told us that families in South America go together to visit the grave of a loved one. Sometimes they bring a meal to share and celebrate the life of their loved one. At first this seemed odd, but we came to be able to share an occasional meal at Bob's grave. Sometimes Mitch brings his guitar and plays from his heart.

Whatever happens, we just sit together with our thoughts. . . .

When we go to the cemetery now there are still feelings of loss, of what would or could have been, but there is also a deep sense of gratitude for a life lived, for a man who was kind and gentle, and who is still a presence felt in our lives. Henri guided us with humor and compassion to a place not of darkness and fear but of peace. He taught us how to remember Bob in new ways, with laughter, joy, and open hearts. Now when we visit Bob's grave we remember also Henri, who was our kind and gentle friend.[59]

Sometimes we grieve not only for a personal friend or loved one, but also for others whom we may have only heard about but who have yet touched our lives. Henri was living in France with Jean Vanier when he wrote this reflection on the grief of a nation who lost a friend and school teacher in Christa McAuliffe, along with the other astronauts who died in the space shuttle Challenger. In speaking about grief, however, he is also aware of the underlying lessons which have the potential to be taught not only for Christa's students but also for all of humanity.

The national grief for the death of the seven astronauts will be fruitful if it helps us to die to our vainglory and our national desire to be the best and the most powerful at all costs, and stimulates us to search for a way of peace not dependent on military superiority. Christa McAuliffe stepped into the Challenger in the hope of teaching her children something new about the universe in which they live. The real challenge now will be to help these children understand and accept without fear the brokenness and mortality of their parents, their teachers, their heroes, and themselves. If this tragedy gradually helps them to love themselves and the adults who guide them as precious, extremely vulnerable, mortal human beings, they may become peacemakers for whom solidarity and compassion are greater gifts than technical genius and the ability to dominate others.[60]

I am not sure that enough of these lessons have been learned, as there continues to be domination in our world, where compassion is sorely called for. Yet, Henri, who believed in the eternal virtues of compassion and peace, uses his faith in humanity and in the eternal love of our creator, God, to illustrate for us the possibilities that lie before us. His words capture the lessons found in the chapters of this book, in a way that can speak to all of us. After watching an IMAX film titled *The Blue Planet* of a view from the space shuttle, Henri reflected on the need for all of us to live and die with a deeper knowledge of being children of one God, and brothers and sisters of one another.

As we look at that beautiful, majestic, blue planet as our home, we suddenly have a completely new understanding of the word our. Our means all people, from all the continents, of all colors, religions, races, and ages. Seen from the space shuttle, the many differences among people that cause hatred, violence, war, oppression, starvation, and mutual destruction seem ridiculous. From the distance of the space shuttle, it is crystal clear that we have the same home, that we belong together, that together we must care for our beautiful blue planet so that we will be able to live here, not just now, but for the long future. Our space age has made it possible for us to grow into a new consciousness of the basic unity of all people on earth and the common responsibility of all people to care for each other and, together, for our home. Seeing our blue planet from a distance, we can say in a new way, "We are indeed brothers and sisters, as Jesus told us long ago. We all are born as fragile beings; we all die as fragile beings. We need each other and our beautifully-made home to live well and to die well."

The distant view of our home may make it possible for us to live and die with a deeper knowledge of being children of one God and brothers and sisters of each other and to truly care.[61]

CONCLUSION

It may seem surprising that we have spent so much time and energy discussing death and dying and have said so little about resurrection. However, Henri addresses it as he concludes *Our Greatest Gift*, explaining that it is actually more important than any of the other things he had written about in that book! He refers to the resurrection as the foundation of his faith. "To write about dying and death without mentioning the resurrection is like writing about sailing without mentioning the wind. The resurrection of Jesus and the hope of our own resurrection have made it possible for me to write about dying and death in the way that I have."[1] He adds some very important insights into trying to comprehend this mystery of our faith.

> The resurrection does not solve our problems about dying and death. It is not the happy ending to our life's struggle, nor is it the big surprise that God has kept in store for us. No, the resurrection is the expression of God's faithfulness to Jesus and to all God's children. Through the resurrection, God has said to Jesus, "You are indeed my beloved Son, and my love is everlasting," and to us God has said, "You indeed are my beloved children, and my love is everlasting." The resurrection is God's way of revealing to us that nothing that belongs to God will ever go to waste. What belongs to God will never get lost—not even our mortal bodies. The resurrection doesn't answer any of our curious questions about life after death, such as, How will it be? How will it look? But it does reveal to us that, indeed, love is stronger than death. After that revelation, we must remain silent, leave the whys, wheres, hows, and whens behind, and simply trust.[2]

And so, we have returned to the notion of the ultimate spiritual task of letting go, and being able to implicitly "trust the Catcher," as Henri would say.

In the introduction to *Our Greatest Gift*, Henri explained that he wanted to die well, but he also desired to help others die well. He wanted his desire to embrace his own mortality help others to embrace theirs. I believe he has certainly been successful. Robert Jonas, one of Henri's friends, writes about how this happened not only through the proliferation of Henri's writings, but how it also began to take place while Henri lived, and particularly through Henri's death. Jonas writes about his own reaction after receiving a phone call early on the morning of September 21, 1996, giving him the sad and shocking news that a second heart attack had taken his friend's life.

> Somehow, in spite of my deep desire that Henri live, in spite of my earnest prayers that he be healed, I had accepted that his death was near. . . .
>
> On another level, I thought that perhaps Henri had prepared his friends well, just as Jesus had. Most of Henri's sermons and books in the last years of his life included reflections on his imminent death. Jesus had taught Henri that life becomes fruitful only when death is faced and folded into our lives, like yeast into a loaf of bread. In his last years, Henri had gradually become transformed into a baker in God's kitchen, working the yeast of death and eternity into every dimension of his life.
>
> Henri had repeated and lived into the words of Jesus' farewell address so often, that now, in my heart, I could not distinguish Jesus' voice from Henri's:
>
> *Do not let your heart be troubled. . . . In my Father's house there are many dwelling places, and now I go to prepare a place for you. . . . Believe me that now, I am in Abba and Abba is in me. . . . I will not leave you orphaned.*[3]

Along with Jonas and others, my own personal life has also been greatly affected by Henri's words and writings. Through this project, I believe I have been called to respond to the challenge Sue Mosteller posed at Henri's funeral: Now he has left us and it is the time for us to take responsibility for the spirituality he gave us. Even before this project was completed, the fruitfulness of Henri's life and writings had already brought insight and comfort to new readers. My mother, Helen, reviewed this manuscript as she sat for days holding the hand of a dying friend. My friend Maureen, who has been nursing cancer patients for thirty years, was also reviewing this work for me when her own husband was faced with the diagnosis of a serious form of cancer. Both women shared with me how reading and reflecting on Henri's writings during that time gave them strength.

Ron Rolheiser, a well-known contemporary spiritual writer, has also described how Henri had a way of being able to reach out to all people.

His life and his writings touched people in all walks of life and not just inside church circles. His approach was deliberate and faith-filled; he was trying to speak to the heart of secular culture from the perspective of the gospel. Slowly, through many years of writing, he developed his own language. He re-wrote his books many times over in an attempt to be simple without being simplistic; to carry real feeling without falling into sentimentality; to speak the language of the soul without falling into psychological jargon; to be personal without being exhibitionist; to put forth Christ's invitation and challenge without being preachy; to challenge the community without being churchy; and to offer God's consolation without falling into mushy piety.

He didn't always succeed, but he did it better than the rest of us. And more so even than the popularity of his writings (that unique appeal and effectiveness of the language he developed) Nouwen is a model to us in terms of the quality of his faith. . . . In the end, what shone through was faith, his belief that God's existence is real and is the most important thing of all.[4]

We don't all walk the same spiritual paths, and it is often difficult to address issues of faith without feeling like we are becoming too personal with our patients or clients. It is sometimes easier with family members or friends, but not always. Yet all of us are longing for wholeness, are longing to be loved, accepted, and valued for who we are, not just what we have accomplished. In understanding how much spiritual wholeness plays a part in wellness, along with the health of the mind and body, we owe it to those we journey with to address their fears and beliefs, and to help them find answers to some of their spiritual questions. Perhaps they can find comfort in Henri's writings, or will feel more at ease addressing these questions with someone who has befriended their own death and explored their own feelings about dying. Henri had a unique way of bridging the spiritual and the secular worlds. This is so often difficult for us to do. However, we need not be afraid to share his writings with others. This allows Henri the opportunity to begin the conversation. Then, trust the Spirit and "The Catcher" to do the rest!

SOURCES CITED

Books

Bernardin, Joseph Cardinal. *The Gift of Peace: Personal Reflections by Joseph Cardinal Bernardin.* Chicago: Loyola Press, 1997.

Beumer, Jurjen. *Henri Nouwen: A Restless Seeking for God.* New York: Crossroad, 1997. (Originally published in Dutch.)

Callanan, Maggie, and Patricia Kelley. *Final Gifts: Understanding the Special Awareness, Needs, and Communications of the Dying.* New York: Bantam Books, 1993.

Ferris, Frank D., Heather M. Balfour, Karen Bowen, Justine Farley, Marsha Hardwick, Claude Lamontagne, Marilyn Lundy, Ann Syme, and Pamela J. West. *A Model to Guide Hospice Palliative Care: Based on National Principles and Norms of Practice.* Ottawa: Canadian Hospice Palliative Care Association, 2002.

Ford, Michael. *Wounded Prophet: A Portrait of Henri J. M. Nouwen.* New York: Doubleday, 1999.

Gaffney, Walter J., and Henri J. M. Nouwen. *Aging.* New York: Doubleday, 1974.

Hillesum, Etty. *An Interrupted Life: The Diaries of Etty Hillesum, 1941–1943.* New York: Pantheon Books, 1983. (Originally published in Dutch.)

Kuhl, David, MD. *What Dying People Want: Practical Wisdom for the End of Life.* Anchor Canada, 2003.

LaNoue, Deirdre. *The Spiritual Legacy of Henri Nouwen.* New York: Continuum, 2000.

McNeill, Donald P., Douglas A. Morrison, and Henri J. M. Nouwen. *Compassion: A Reflection on the Christian Life.* New York: Doubleday, 1983. Rev. ed., 2005.

Nouwen, Henri J. M. *Adam: God's Beloved.* Maryknoll, NY: Orbis Books, 1997.

———. *Beyond the Mirror.* New York: Crossroad, 1990.

———. *Bread for the Journey: A Daybook of Wisdom and Faith.* San Francisco: HarperCollins, 1997.

———. *Can You Drink the Cup?* Notre Dame: Ave Maria Press, 1996.

———. *A Cry For Mercy: Prayers from the Genesee.* New York: Doubleday, 1981.

———. *Finding My Way Home.* New York: Crossroad Publishing, 2001

———. *The Genesee Diary: Report from a Trappist Monastery.* New York: Doubleday, 1976.

———. *¡Gracias!: A Latin American Journal.* San Francisco: Harper and Row, 1983.

———. *Henri Nouwen: Writings.* Selected with an introduction by Robert A. Jonas. Maryknoll, NY: Orbis Books, 1998.

———. *Here and Now: Living in the Spirit.* New York: Crossroad, 1994.

———. *In Memoriam.* Notre Dame: Ave Maria Press, 1980.

———. *The Inner Voice of Love: A Journey through Anguish to Freedom.* New York: Doubleday, 1996.

———. *Jesus: A Gospel.* Edited and introduced by Michael O'Laughlin. Maryknoll, NY: Orbis Books, 2001.

———. *A Letter of Consolation.* San Francisco: Harper and Row, 1982.

———. *Letters to Marc about Jesus.* San Francisco: Harper and Row, 1988.

———. *Life of the Beloved: Spiritual Living in a Secular World.* New York: Crossroad, 1992.

———. *Lifesigns: Intimacy, Fecundity, and Ecstasy in Christian Perspective.* Garden City, NY: Doubleday, 1986; reprint, 2003.

———. *The Living Reminder: Service and Prayer in Memory of Jesus Christ.* New York: Harper Collins, 1977.

———. *Love in a Fearful Land: A Guatemalan Story.* Notre Dame: Ave Maria Press, 1985. Rev. ed. Maryknoll, NY: Orbis Books, 2006.

———. *Making All Things New: An Invitation to the Spiritual Life.* New York: Harper and Row, 1981.

————. *Our Greatest Gift: A Meditation on Dying and Caring*. San Francisco: HarperCollins, 1994.

————. *Out of Solitude: Three Meditations on the Christian Life*. Notre Dame: Ave Maria Press, 1974. Rev. ed., 2004.

————. *Peacework: Prayer, Resistance, Community*. Maryknoll, NY: Orbis Books, 2005.

————. *Reaching Out: The Three Movements of the Spiritual Life*. New York: Doubleday, 1975.

————. *The Return of the Prodigal Son*. New York: Doubleday Image Books, 1992.

————. *The Road to Daybreak: A Spiritual Journey*. New York: Doubleday Image Books, 1988.

————. *Sabbatical Journey: The Diary of His Final Year*. New York: Crossroad, 1998.

————. *Spiritual Direction: Wisdom for the Long Walk of Faith*. With Michael J. Christensen and Rebecca J. Laird. San Francisco: HarperSanFrancisco, 2006.

————. *Turn My Mourning into Dancing: Finding Hope in Hard Times*. Compiled and edited by Timothy Jones. Nashville, TN: Thomas Nelson Co., 2001.

————. *The Way of the Heart: Desert Spirituality and Contemporary Ministry*. New York: Seabury Press, 1981.

O'Laughlin, Michael. *God's Beloved: A Spiritual Biography of Henri Nouwen*. Maryknoll, NY: Orbis Books, 2004.

————. *Henri Nouwen: His Life and Vision*. Maryknoll, NY: Orbis Books, 2005.

Porter, Beth, with Susan M. S. Brown and Philip Coulter, eds. *Befriending Life: Encounters with Henri Nouwen*. New York: Doubleday, 2001.

Powell, Jane. "Grieving in the Context of a Community of Differently-Abled People: The Experience of L'Arche Daybreak" in *Complicated Grieving and Bereavement: Understanding and Treating People Experiencing Loss*, ed. Gerry Cox, Robert A. Bendiksen, and Robert Stevenson. Amityville, NY: Baywood, 2002.

Rolheiser, Ronald. *The Holy Longing: The Search for a Christian Spirituality*. New York: Doubleday, 1999.

Schwartz, Morrie. *Morrie: In His Own Words*. New York: Dell, 1996. (Previously printed as *Letting Go*.)

Smith, Harold Ivan. *Finding Your Way to Say Goodbye: Comfort for the Dying and Those Who Care for Them*. Notre Dame: Ave Maria Press, 2002.

Articles

Nouwen, Henri. "For Henri Nouwen, Death Not So Mortal." *National Catholic Reporter* (1 April 1994): 11–12.

Unpublished Manuscripts

Nouwen, Henri. "On Departure." 12 May 1968. Henri J. M. Nouwen Archives and Research Collection, John M. Kelly Library, University of St. Michael's College, Toronto.

Speeches, Addresses, Homilies

Nouwen, Henri. "A Time to Mourn, A Time to Dance." Address made at Christian Counseling Services 25th Celebration, 4 February1992; excerpts subsequently published in *Turn My Mourning Into Dancing*.

————. "Befriending Death." Address made at the National Catholic AIDS Ministry Conference, Chicago, July 1995. Henri J. M. Nouwen Archives & Research Collection, John M. Kelly Library, University of St. Michael's College, Toronto; excerpts subsequently published in *Finding My Way Home*.

Interviews

Argan, Glen. "Nouwen Finds a Home: Theologian Moved in with the Handicapped." Interview. *Western Catholic Reporter*, 21 March 1994.

Lywood, Wendy. Interviewed by Michelle O'Rourke. Written notes. Richmond Hill, Ontario. 17 September 2007.

"Henri Nouwen on Death and Aging." Interview. *Cross Point* (Fall 1995): 1–8.

Videocassettes

Nouwen, Henri. *Angels over the Net*. Prod. Isabelle Steyart and dir. Bart

Gavigan. 30 min. Spark Productions, 1995.

———. *Interview with Henri Nouwen.* University of Notre Dame Alumni, Continuing Education. 3 April 1996. Henri J. M. Nouwen Archives and Research Collection, John M. Kelly Library, University of St. Michael's College, Toronto.

———. *Journey of the Heart: The Life of Henri Nouwen.* Prod./Dir. Karen Pascal. Windborne Productions, Markham, Ontario, 2007.

Internet Sources

Clinton, Hillary. "Hillary Clinton on *The Return of the Prodigal Son.*" *O, The Oprah Magazine,* July/August 2000 issue, as archived on Oprah.com.

Davis, Jan. "On the Journey to Seeing with the Eyes of the Heart." Weekly Reflection Series. email_lists@henrinouwen.org. 5 March 2008.

Mosteller, Sue. "On the Journey toward Aging Gracefully." Weekly Reflection Series. email_lists@henrinouwen.org. 14 November 2007.

Ontario Palliative Care Association. *Mission Statement.* Home Page. http://www.ontariopalliativecare.org/main.htm. Accessed 7 November 2007.

Rolheiser, Ronald. *From Maintenance to Missionary.* 14 January 2001. www.ronrolheiser.com.

NOTES

Introduction

[1] www.ontariopalliativecare.org, home page.

[2] Henri Nouwen, *Our Greatest Gift: A Meditation on Dying and Caring* (San Francisco: HarperCollins, 1994), xiv.

[3] Hillary Clinton, "The First Lady on *The Return of the Prodigal Son,*" *O, The Oprah Magazine,* July/August 2000 issue, as archived on Oprah.com.

[4] Henri Nouwen, *Spiritual Direction: Wisdom for the Long Walk of Faith,* with Michael J. Christensen and Rebecca J. Laird (New York: HarperSanFrancisco, 2006), x.

[5] Nouwen, *Our Greatest Gift,* 6.

1. Getting to Know Henri

[1] Michael O'Laughlin, *God's Beloved: A Spiritual Biography of Henri Nouwen* (Maryknoll, NY: Orbis Books, 2004), 12.

[2] Ibid., 34.

[3] Vatican II was a series of conferences held over a four-year period, 1962 to 1965, during which the pope, bishops from around the world, and other church leaders examined the Catholic Church's structure, teachings, liturgical practices, and relevance in the modern world, initiating many fundamental changes.

[4] Jurjen Beumer, *Henri Nouwen: A Restless Seeking for God* (New York: Crossroad, 1997), 27.

[5] O'Laughlin, *God's Beloved,* 49–50.

[6] Beumer, *Henri Nouwen,* 28.

[7] Ibid., 30.

[8] Michael O'Laughlin, *Henri Nouwen: His Life and Vision* (Maryknoll, NY: Orbis Books, 2005), 61.

[9] Henri Nouwen, *Reaching Out: The Three Movements of the Spiritual Life* (New York: Doubleday, 1975), 13.

[10] O'Laughlin, *Henri Nouwen,* 64.

[11] Ibid., 69.

[12]*Henri Nouwen: Writings*, selected with an introduction by Robert A. Jonas, Modern Spiritual Masters Series (Maryknoll, NY: Orbis Books, 1998), xxxiii.

[13]Ibid., xxxiv.

[14]Henri Nouwen, *¡Gracias! A Latin American Journal* (San Francisco: Harper and Row, 1983), 188.

[15]Henri Nouwen, *The Road to Daybreak: A Spiritual Journey* (New York: Doubleday, 1988), 9.

[16]O'Laughlin, *Henri Nouwen*, 106.

[17]Beumer, *Henri Nouwen*, 56.

[18]Nouwen, *The Road to Daybreak*, 43.

[19]Ibid., 94–95.

[20]Henri Nouwen, *In Memoriam* (Notre Dame: Ave Maria Press, 1980), 10–11.

[21]Ibid., 60.

[22]Ibid., 36.

[23]Henri Nouwen, *A Letter of Consolation* (New York: Harper and Row, 1982), 19.

[24]Henri Nouwen, *Adam: God's Beloved* (Maryknoll, NY: Orbis Books, 1997), 41.

[25]Ibid., 43.

[26]Ibid., 50.

[27]Ibid., 101.

[28]Ibid., 10–11.

[29]Henri Nouwen, *The Inner Voice of Love: A Journey through Anguish to Freedom* (New York: Doubleday, 1996), xiii–xvi.

[30]Ibid., xvi–xvii.

[31]Ibid., xvii.

[32]Henri Nouwen, *Beyond the Mirror* (New York: Crossroad, 1990), 28.

[33]Ibid., 34–37.

[34]Ibid., 9.

[35]Henri Nouwen, *Sabbatical Journey: The Diary of His Final Year* (New York: Crossroad, 1998), 51.

[36]Ibid., 93.

[37]Ibid., 170.

[38]Nouwen, *Our Greatest Gift*, 44–45.

[39]Nouwen, *Beyond the Mirror*, 12.

[40]Ibid., 66.

[41]Ibid., 59.

[42]Deirdre LaNoue, *The Spiritual Legacy of Henri Nouwen* (New York: Continuum, 2000), 152–153.

2. Nouwen's Spirituality

[1]Sue Mosteller, quoted in Michael Ford, *Wounded Prophet: A Portrait of Henri J. M. Nouwen* (New York: Doubleday, 1999), 205–206.

[2]LaNoue, *The Spiritual Legacy of Henri Nouwen*, 2, quoting *HarperCollins Encyclopedia of Catholicism*, s.v. "Christian Spirituality," 1216.

[3]Henri Nouwen, *The Return of the Prodigal Son* (New York: Doubleday Image Books, 1992), 134.

[4]Ibid., 98–99.

[5]Ibid., 105–106.

[6]Ibid., 106.

[7]Ibid., 105.

[8]LaNoue, *The Spiritual Legacy of Henri Nouwen*, 63.

[9]Henri Nouwen, *Bread for the Journey: A Daybook of Wisdom and Faith* (San Francisco: HarperCollins, 1997), February 5th notation (page numbers not present in this edition; dates are used only for reference).

[10]Henri Nouwen, *Letters to Marc about Jesus* (San Francisco: Harper and Row, 1987), 55.

[11]Nouwen, *Bread for the Journey*, February 28th notation.

[12]LaNoue, *The Spiritual Legacy of Henri Nouwen*, 58.

[13]Ibid., 81.

[14]Nouwen, *Bread for the Journey*, March 1st and 2nd notations.

[15]Henri Nouwen, *Jesus: A Gospel*, ed. Michael O'Laughlin (Maryknoll, NY: Orbis Books, 2001), xi.

[16]Nouwen, *Letters to Marc about Jesus*, 7.

[17]Henri Nouwen, *Making All Things New: An Invitation to the Spiritual Life* (New York: Harper and Row, 1981), 47.

[18]Nouwen, *Sabbatical Journey*, 177–178.

[19]Henri Nouwen, *Here and Now: Living in the Spirit* (New York: Crossroad, 1994), 144.

[20]Nouwen, *The Road to Daybreak*, 100–101.

[21]Nouwen, *The Inner Voice of Love*, 57.

[22]Henri Nouwen, *Can You Drink the Cup?* (Notre Dame: Ave Maria Press, 1996), 63–64.

[23] Ibid., 64.

[24]Karen Pascal, *Journey of the Heart: The Life of Henri Nouwen* (Markham, Ontario: Windborne Productions, 2007), video recording.

[25]Nouwen, *Making All Things New,* 87.

[26]Glen Argan, "Nouwen Finds a Home," *Western Catholic Reporter,* 21 March 1994, 6.

[27]Donald P. McNeill, Douglas A. Morrison, and Henri Nouwen, *Compassion: A Reflection on the Christian Life* (New York: Doubleday, 1982; rev. ed., 2005), 81 (page citations are to the revised edition).

[28]Nouwen, *The Road to Daybreak,* 164.

[29]Nouwen, *Making All Things New,* 88.

[30]Ibid., 90.

[31]Henri Nouwen, *Out of Solitude* (Notre Dame: Ave Maria Press, 1974; rev. ed., 2004), 26 (citations are to the revised edition).

[32]Nouwen, *¡Gracias!,* 20–21.

[33]Henri Nouwen, *The Way of the Heart: Desert Spirituality and Contemporary Ministry* (New York: Seabury Press, 1981), 40.

[34] Ibid., 26.

[35]Ibid., 33–34.

[36]Nouwen, *The Return of the Prodigal Son,* 126.

[37]Nouwen, *Here and Now,* 104–105.

[38]McNeill, Morrison, and Nouwen, *Compassion,* 39.

[39]Ibid., 37.

[40]Ibid., 29.

[41]Jan Davis, "On the Journey to Seeing with the Eyes of the Heart," from the Henri Nouwen Society Weekly Reflections, 5 March 2008, available from henrinouwen.org.

3. Befriending Death

[1]Nouwen, *A Letter of Consolation,* 29–30.

[2]Ibid., 31.

[3]Nouwen, *Bread for the Journey,* April 17th notation.

[4]Nouwen, *A Letter of Consolation,* 32.

[5]Ibid., 33–35.

[6]Nouwen, *Here and Now,* 134.

[7]Ibid., 135.

[8]Henri Nouwen, "Befriending Death" (transcript of a presentation at the National Catholic AIDS Network, Chicago, Illinois, July 1995), Henri J. M. Nouwen Archives & Research Collection, John M. Kelly Library, University of St. Michael's College,

Toronto, 5.

[9]Ibid., 6.

[10]Henri Nouwen, *Life of the Beloved* (New York: Crossroad, 1992), 106.

[11]Ibid.

[12]Nouwen, *Letters to Marc about Jesus,* 7.

[13]Ibid., 5.

[14]Nouwen, *Sabbatical Journey,* 165.

[15]Nouwen, *¡Gracias!,* 44.

[16]Nouwen, *Here and Now,* 136–137.

[17]Henri Nouwen, *Love in a Fearful Land: A Guatemalan Story* (Notre Dame: Ave Maria Press, 1985; rev. ed., Maryknoll, NY: Orbis Books, 2006), 103 (page citations are to the revised edition).

[18]Nouwen, *The Road to Daybreak,* 116–117.

[19]Henri Nouwen, *A Cry for Mercy: Prayers from the Genesee* (New York: Doubleday, 1981), 93.

[20]Nouwen, *¡Gracias!,* 59.

[21]Ibid., 58.

[22]Nouwen, *Here and Now,* 89.

[23]Nouwen, "Befriending Death," 6.

[24]Nouwen, *Our Greatest Gift,* 47.

[25]Ibid., 24.

[26]Ibid., 25.

[27]Ibid., 26.

[28]Ibid., 4.

[28]Ibid., 31.

[30]Ibid., 29.

[31]Ibid., 35–36.

[32]Ibid., 36.

[33]Ibid., 37.

[34]Henri Nouwen, *The Living Reminder* (San Francisco: Harper Collins, 1977), 39–41.

[35]Henri Nouwen, *Lifesigns: Intimacy, Fecundity, and Ecstasy in Christian Perspective* (Garden City, NY: Doubleday, 1986; reprint 2003), 44 (page citations are from reprint edition).

[36]Nouwen, *Our Greatest Gift,* xv–xvi.

[37]Nouwen, *Bread for the Journey,* November 29th notation.

[38]Ibid., December 6th notation.

[39]Nouwen, *Our Greatest Gift,* xvi–xvii.

[40]Ibid., 19-20

4. Dying Well

[1]Frank Ferris et al., eds., *A Model to Guide Hospice Palliative Care: Based on National Principles and Norms of Practice* (Ottawa: Canadian Hospice Palliative

Care Association, 2002), v.

[2]Henri Nouwen, "For Henri Nouwen, Death Not So Mortal," *National Catholic Reporter*, 1 April 1994, 11

[3]Nouwen, *Our Greatest Gift*, 15.

[4]Ibid., 14–15.

[5]Walter Gaffney and Henri Nouwen, *Aging* (New York: Doubleday, 1974), 4.

[6]Sue Mosteller, "On the Journey toward Aging Gracefully," from the Henri Nouwen Society Weekly Reflection, 14 November 2007, available from henrinouwen.org.

[7]Henri Nouwen, "Henri Nouwen on Death and Aging," *Cross Point* (Fall 1995), 2.

[8]Ibid.

[9]Ibid., 4.

[10]Ibid.

[11]Nouwen, "Befriending Death," 7.

[12]Henri Nouwen, "On Departure," 12 May 1968, Manuscript Series, Henri J. M. Nouwen Archives and Research Collection, John M. Kelly Library, University of St. Michael's College, Toronto, 2.

[13]Henri Nouwen, "A Time to Mourn, A Time to Dance," 1992, Manuscript Series, Henri J. M. Nouwen Archives and Research Collection, John M. Kelly Library, University of St. Michael's College, Toronto, 8.

[14]Ibid., 14.

[15]Nouwen, *The Road to Daybreak*, 160–161.

[16]Henri Nouwen, *The Genesee Diary: Report from a Trappist Monastery* (New York: Doubleday, 1976), 157.

[17]McNeill, Morrison, and Nouwen, *Compassion*, 38.

[18]Nouwen, *Here and Now*, 33.

[19]Nouwen, "A Time to Mourn, A Time to Dance," 16–17.

[20]Ibid., 18.

[21]Ibid., 18–19.

[22]Ibid., 19.

[23]Nouwen, *Beyond the Mirror*, 38–42.

[24]Nouwen, *Bread for the Journey*, August 27th notation

[25]Nouwen, "A Time to Mourn, A Time to Dance," 23–24.

[26]Nouwen, *The Road to Daybreak*, 20–21.

[27]Nouwen, "A Time to Mourn, A Time to Dance," 25–26.

[28]Nouwen, *The Return of the Prodigal Son*, 85.

[29]Nouwen, *Bread for the Journey*, August 28th notation.

[30]Nouwen, "A Time to Mourn, A Time to Dance," 27–28.

[31]Nouwen, *Lifesigns*, 56.

[32]Nouwen, *Our Greatest Gift*, 17–18.

[33]Nouwen, *The Inner Voice of Love*, 91–92.

[34]McNeill, Morrison, and Nouwen, *Compassion*, 41–42.

[35]Nouwen, *The Return of the Prodigal Son*, 121.

[36]Henri Nouwen, *Angels over the Net* (1995), video recording; viewed at the Henri J. M. Nouwen Archives and Research Collection, John M. Kelly Library, University of St. Michael's College, Toronto.

[37]Nouwen, "Befriending Death," 8.

[38]Ibid., 8–9.

[39]Ibid., 9–10.

[40]Nouwen, *Bread for the Journey*, December 7th notation.

5. Caring Well

[1] Nouwen, *Out of Solitude*, 37–38.

[2]Ibid., 39.

[3]Ibid., 38.

[4] Nouwen, *Here and Now*, 106–107.

[5]Beth Porter, with Susan M. S. Brown and Philip Coulter, eds., *Befriending Life: Encounters with Henri Nouwen* (New York: Doubleday, 2001), xix.

[6]Ibid., 29, 33.

[7]Nouwen, *Bread for the Journey*, February 8th notation.

[8]Nouwen, *Beyond the Mirror*, 71–72.

[9]Nouwen, *Here and Now*, 107.

[10]David Kuhl, M.D., *What Dying People Want: Practical Wisdom for the End of Life* (Canada: Anchor Canada, 2002), xv.

[11]Ibid., 28–29.

[12]Maggie Callanan and Patricia Kelley, *Final Gifts: Understanding the Special Awareness, Needs, and Communications of the Dying* (New York: Bantam Books, 1992), 67.

[13]Morrie Schwartz, *Morrie: In His Own Words*, previously published as *Letting Go*

(New York: Dell, 1996), 77.

[14]Nouwen, *Letters to Marc about Jesus,* 29–30.

[15]Porter et al., *Befriending Life,* 233.

[16]Ibid., 234.

[17]Wendy Lywood, interview by Michelle O'Rourke, Daybreak, Richmond Hill, Ontario, 17 September 2007.

[18]Porter et al., *Befriending Life,* 235.

[19]Joseph Cardinal Bernardin, *The Gift of Peace: Personal Reflections by Joseph Cardinal Bernardin* (Chicago: Loyola Press, 1997), 127–128.

[20]Jane Powell, "Grieving in the Context of a Community of Differently-Abled People: The Experience of L'Arche Daybreak," as found in *Complicated Grieving and Bereavement: Understanding and Treating People Experiencing Loss,* ed. Gerry Cox, Robert A. Bendiksen, and Robert Stevenson (Amityville, NY: Baywood, 2002), 123.

[21]Callanan and Kelley, *Final Gifts,* 159.

[22]Nouwen, *Bread for the Journey,* May 19th notation.

[23]Ibid., December 5th notation.

[24]McNeill, Morrison, and Nouwen, *Compassion,* 3.

[25]Nouwen, *Here and Now,* 98–99.

[26]McNeill, Morrison, and Nouwen, *Compassion,* 88.

[27]Nouwen, *Out of Solitude,* 41–42.

[28]Nouwen, *¡Gracias!,* 18.

[29]Nouwen, *The Living Reminder,* 24–25.

[30]Nouwen, *Lifesigns,* 30–31.

[31]Ibid., 35.

[32]Henri Nouwen, *Peacework: Prayer, Resistance, Community* (New York: Orbis Books, 2005), 36.

[33]Nouwen, *Out of Solitude,* 25.

[34]Nouwen, *The Living Reminder,* 34.

[35]Nouwen, *Here and Now,* 93–94.

[36]Nouwen, *The Living Reminder,* 34.

[37]Nouwen, *Letters to Marc about Jesus,* 84.

[38]Ibid., 34.

[39]Etty Hillesum, *An Interrupted Life: The Diaries of Etty Hillesum, 1941–1943* (New York: Pantheon Books, 1983), 185.

[40]Nouwen, *Here and Now,* 144.

[41]Nouwen, *Sabbatical Journey,* 109.

[42]Nouwen, *Here and Now,* 102–103.

[43]Ibid., 109–110.

[44]Interview with Henri Nouwen, University of Notre Dame Alumni, Continuing Education, 3 April 1996, video recording; viewed at the Henri J. M. Nouwen Archives and Research Collection, John M. Kelly Library, University of St. Michael's College, Toronto.

[45]Nouwen, *The Inner Voice of Love,* 7.

[46]McNeill, Morrison, and Nouwen, *Compassion,* 59.

[47]Nouwen, *Our Greatest Gift,* 58–63.

[48]Nouwen, *Adam,* 90.

[49]Nouwen, *Our Greatest Gift,* 95.

[50]Nouwen, *Our Greatest Gift,* 96–97.

[51]Porter et al., *Befriending Life,* 108.

[52]Harold Ivan Smith, *Finding Your Way to Say Goodbye: Comfort for the Dying and Those Who Care for Them* (Notre Dame: Ave Maria Press, 2002), 15–16.

[53]Ibid., 22.

[54]Nouwen, *Bread for the Journey,* August 26th notation.

[55]Nouwen, *A Cry for Mercy,* 68–69.

[56]Porter et al., *Befriending Life,* 235–236.

[57]Powell, "Grieving in the Context of a Community of Differently-Abled People," 131.

[58]Porter et al., *Befriending Life,* 236–237.

[59]Ibid., 120–121.

[60]Nouwen, *The Road to Daybreak,* 130.

[61]Nouwen, *Our Greatest Gift,* 84–85.

Conclusion

[1]Nouwen, *Our Greatest Gift,* 106.

[2]Ibid., 108-109.

[3]Jonas, *Henri Nouwen,* xx–xxi.

[4]Ron Rolheiser, *From Maintenance to Missionary* (www.ronrolheiser.com: archive article, 14 January 2001).